PAPUA NEW GUINEA

Language in context

Grade 5 Student Book

Tandi Jackson

Illustrated by Jeanette Baude

OXFORD

Level 8, 737 Bourke Street, Docklands, Victoria 3008, Australia

Oxford University Press is a department of the University of Oxford. It furthers the University's objective of excellence in research, scholarship, and education by publishing worldwide in

Oxford New York

Auckland Cape Town Dar es Salaam Hong Kong Karachi Kuala Lumpur Madrid Melbourne Mexico City Nairobi New Delhi Shanghai Taipei Toronto

With offices in

Argentina Austria Brazil Chile Czech Republic France Greece Guatemala Hungary Italy Japan Poland Portugal Singapore South Korea Switzerland Thailand Turkey Ukraine Vietnam

First published 2008

Reprinted 2008 (twice), 2009, 2010, 2013, 2014 (twice), 2016 (twice), 2017, 2024 (D)

ISBN 978 0 19 556065 7

Typeset by Polar Design Pty Ltd
Illustrated by Jeanette Baude
Maps By MAPGraphics Pty Ltd
Printed and bound in Australia by Ligare Book Printers Pty Ltd

Acknowledgments

The author and publisher wish to thank the following copyright holders for granting permission to reproduce their material.
AAP Image/Lloyd Jones, pp. 18, 19; AAP Image/Rocky Roe, pp. 3 bottom left, 19 top left; Corbis/Brooks Kraft, p. 3 top left; Newspix/Auri Eva, pp. 3 right, 19 bottom; Photolibrary/Photo Researchers, p. 69.

Every effort has been made to trace the original source of copyright material contained in this book. The publisher would be pleased to hear from copyright holders to rectify any errors or omissions.

Contents

Introduction

This year Kali introduces your work.

- ✓ Remember not to write in this book.
- ✓ Keep your hands clean when using it.
- ✓ Write down all your answers in an exercise book.
- ✓ Before writing your answers, think carefully about the question. You may have to refer to other pages or maps to find your answer.

Making Good Decisions for our Country

Chapter summary

In this chapter you will:

- ✓ Learn about our government
- ✓ Learn about how we vote for a new government
- ✓ Learn about law and order in this country
- ✓ Learn about traditional leadership and leadership today
- ✓ Learn about women in politics today
- ✓ Learn about how the government provides goods and services
- ✓ Learn about problems faced by the government.

Cross-curriculum topics

These topics apply only to this chapter.

Topic: Community living

Strand: Community

Sub-strand: People

5.1.1 Analyse people's contributions to the community.

Sub-strand: Ways communities work

5.1.3 Describe democratic and traditional decision-making processes – how leaders are chosen.

Strand: Trading

Sub-strand: Meeting wants and needs

5.2.1 Analyse the distribution of goods and services.

Our government system

Papua New Guinea is a **constitutional monarchy**.

This means that the **Queen** of England (the **monarch**) is the head of our country.

We have a **constitution** (set of rules) that tells how our country will be governed.

The **Governor-general** is the Queen's representative. This means that because the Queen does not live in PNG the Governor-General does things in her place.

The **Prime Minister** is the head of the government. He is **elected** (chosen) by the members of parliament.

The people vote and elect **members of parliament** to be in the government.

The Queen

The Governor-General

The Prime Minister

There are three levels of government in PNG. There is **national parliament** in Port Moresby, **provincial governments** in the provinces and **local level governments** at the village level.

Put these in the correct order:

Local level government
Prime Minister
Queen Elizabeth II
National parliament
Governor-General
Provincial government

Find out who the prime minister is.

Find out who the governor-general is.

New words to learn

Parliament is the name for the members who represent the people.

An **elector** is a person who can vote in an election. He/she must be over 18.

Electorates are the places or districts that the country is divided into for voting.

Elections are the times when people vote.

Elected is when people vote for a person and he/she joins Parliament.

National means about the whole country.

Provincial means about a province.

Voting means to choose someone that you want to be your representative in parliament.

A **Member of Parliament** is a person who has been elected to Parliament.

A **secret ballot** is a secret vote where no one else can see who you're voting for.

The **constitution** contains the rules of the country. It says how the country will be governed.

National parliament

Members of Parliament are elected from 19 provinces and the National Capital District of Port Moresby.

Each province is divided into districts.

Parliament is made up of **89** electorates (one from each district) and **20** regional electorates (one from each province).

Each of these regional members is also the **provincial governor**.

Each province is responsible for looking after its own affairs.

Find out who your provincial governor is.

Finish these sentences:

1 National parliament is made up of a total of __________ electorates.

2 Each regional member is also called a ______________________________.

3 Port Moresby is in the __________________________ District.

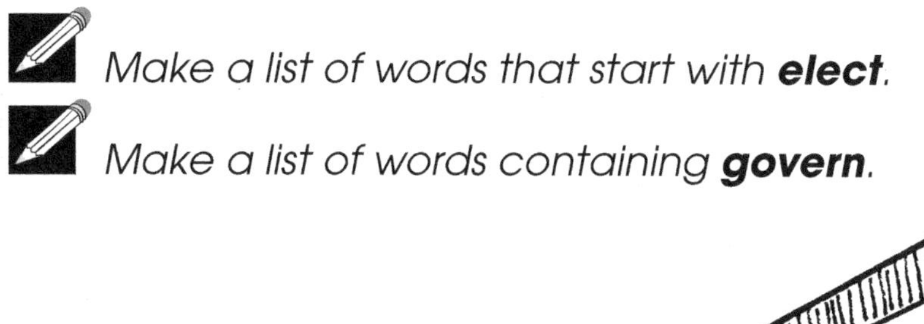

*Make a list of words that start with **elect**.*

*Make a list of words containing **govern**.*

Read **Bird of Paradise**.

Provinces of Papua New Guinea

Using a map, find the capitals of these provinces.

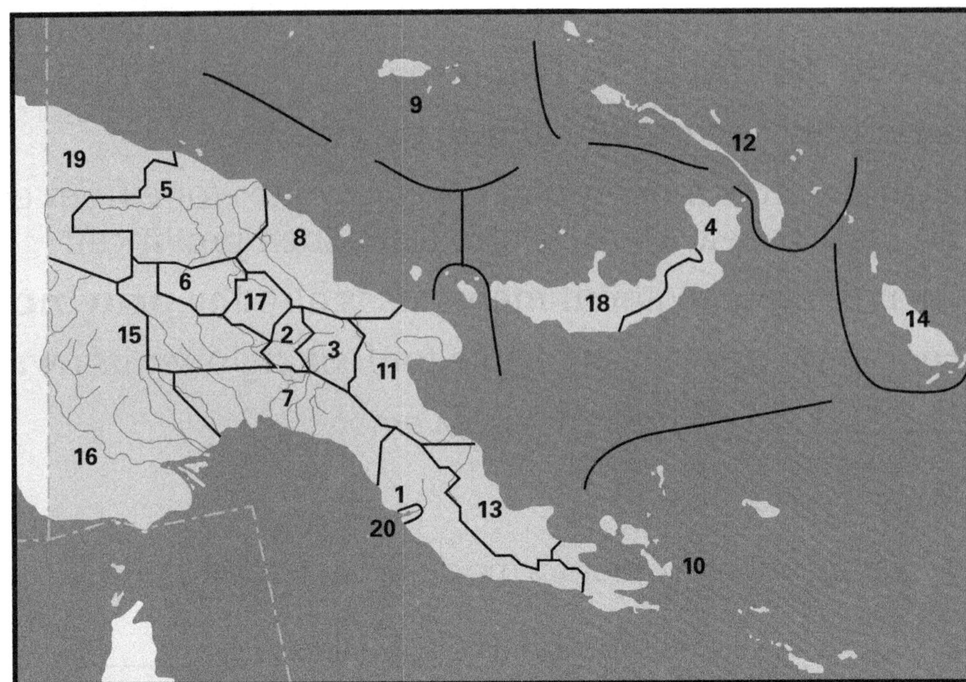

	Province	Area (km²)	Population
1	Central	29 500	161 447
2	Simbu (Chimbu)	6 100	187 809
3	Eastern Highlands	11 200	316 802
4	East New Britain	15 500	235 712
5	East Sepik	42 800	280 340
6	Enga	12 800	279 046
7	Gulf	34 500	72 794
8	Madang	29 000	288 317
9	Manus	2 100	38 697
10	Milne Bay	14 000	185 000
11	Morobe	34 500	439 725
12	New Ireland	9 600	105 893
13	Oro (Northern)	22 800	112 985
14	North Solomons (Bougainville)	9 300	178 262
15	Southern Highlands	23 800	390 240
16	Western	99 300	126 411
17	Western Highlands	8 500	398 376
18	West New Britain	21 000	170 485
19	Sandaun (West Sepik)	36 300	160 349
20	National Capital District	240	271 813

The capital towns of the provinces are listed below. Match them to the correct provinces on page 6.

Port Moresby	Kerema
Kundiawa	Madang
Goroka	Lorengau
Rabaul	Wabag
Wewak	Mendi
Alotou	Daru
Lae	Mount Hagen
Kavieng	Kimbe
Popondetta	Vanimo
Arawa	

1. *Which province has the biggest population?*
2. *How many people live there?*
3. *Which province has the smallest population?*
4. *How many people live there?*
5. *Which province has the biggest area of land? How big is it?*
6. *Which province has the smallest area of land?*
7. *What is another name for the Oro Province?*
8. *What is another name for the West Sepik Province?*
9. *Look at the map and list the provinces that are islands or include islands.*
10. *What is the total population of Madang Province and Manus Province?*
11. *What is the population of your province?*
12. *What is the area of land in your province?*

Draw a map of PNG and draw in the provinces. Shade in the province where you live.

Provincial governments

Provincial governments were made in 1975 to take the power from the centre to the community level where many villages share the same culture.

Local level governments (LLGs)

In 1995, the **New Organic Law** was brought in. This replaced the 19 elected provincial governments with local level governments. This was another way to move power to the local level, giving greater powers to the members of parliament and the local government councils.

District level

Each Province is divided into one or more Districts.

There are a total of 89 Districts.

Each District must plan what to do and how to spend their budget (money).

Local level

Each District is divided into one or more local level governments (LLGs). There are 284 LLGs.

Ward level

Each LLG has many wards. There are 5747 wards in total.

Communities and villages

Each ward is made up of many small villages and non-traditional village areas.

Elections

An election is when people over 18 have the chance to vote. They choose people to represent them in parliament. Elections are held every five years.

Find out when the last election was.

When will the next election be?

Unscramble these words about the government:

etov	wdra
arplmiatne	neecltoi
ttidrsci	uqnee
noinocttuist	

Voting

Fill in the spaces.

1 When it is time to vote it is called an ________________.

2 You have to be ________________ years old to vote.

3 Elections are held every ________________ years.

4 Voting means to ________________ people to represent you.

5 The people with the most ________________ are chosen.

6 These people represent you in ________________.

Up until 2002, for general elections, where members of parliament were elected, a system called **first-past-the-post** was used.

This meant that the first person to get the highest number of votes was elected or chosen.

Since 2002, a method called **limited preferential voting (LPV)** has been used.

This means that the person **voting** must choose a **first**, **second** and **third** choice.

On the next page is an example of an **LPV** voting form.

Elizabeth Angon	2
Maki Besa	1
Alois Bengti	3

Secret ballot

Your vote is secret. It is called a secret ballot. No one can see your voting form.

You should vote for the person that *you* want to be elected.

You should not vote for someone who has bribed you or threatened you.

You have to be 18 years old to vote and you can only vote once in each election.

Hold a secret ballot to elect a class leader.

 *Write a paragraph saying why you think the person you voted for would make a good leader.*

Answer these questions:

1. *What does **LPV** mean?*
2. *Describe a secret ballot.*
3. *How old do you have to be to vote in an election?*
4. *How many votes can you have?*
5. *What does **first-past-the-post** mean?*

Political parties

There are many different political parties in PNG.

This type of party does not mean to sing and dance. A political party is a group of people who have ideas about how to look after and lead the province or country they live in.

Papua New Guinea has a **multi-party** system, with many different parties.

One party is usually not able to be in power on its own. Parties must work with each other to form groups which can govern together. These groups are called **coalition governments**.

The government has **109** members.

The **people** elect the Members of Parliament.

The **Members of Parliament** elect a Prime Minister.

The **Prime Minister** chooses a cabinet from members of his party or a coalition party.

Find out who is the Minister for Finance.

Find out who is the Minister for Health.

Find out who is the Minister for Education.

The constitution

The **constitution** is a document that tells how the country will be run. It contains the rules and the laws of the country and says how the people will be treated. Some of the things it says are about:

- respect for human rights
- protecting the rights of women
- protecting the rights of children
- freedom of speech
- freedom of religion
- respect for political rights.

Match these sentences with the headings above.

1 Children should be given food, clothing and shelter.

2 People should be able to vote for whoever they like.

3 People should be able to choose which religion to follow.

4 Women should be treated with respect and given the same rights as men.

5 All people should be treated well.

6 You should be able to give your opinion on things without fear.

Label these things correctly and copy them into your book.

National emblem
National anthem
National flag
National motto

A

B

C Unity in Diversity

D O arise all ye sons of this land
Let us sing of our joy to be free
Praising God and rejoicing to be
Papa New Guinea.

The justice system

PNG's laws are based on the **constitution**.

When people break the law, they have to go to court and be punished.

There are different courts for different crimes.

- **The Supreme Court** deals with constitutional matters or big conflicts.
- **The National Court** deals with serious criminal matters from the district court like murder, rape and robberies with violence.
- **District courts** deal with lesser criminal matters like breaking and entering, damaging property, stealing and dangerous driving.
- **Family courts** deal with family problems.
- **Village courts** deal with small disputes between village people, such as sorcery, theft, insults, fighting and drunkenness.

Read the examples below and decide which court they should be taken to. Draw a table to put your answers in.

1 The PNG Eco-Forestry Forum has entered a Court Appeal against logging rights being unlawfully granted to foreign logging companies.

2 A woman wants to take her husband to court for beating her.

3 A man is charged with breaking into a shop and stealing some food.

4 A youth is charged with stealing a car.

5 A man is charged with practising sorcery against another man in his village.

6 A young man is charged with insulting a village elder.

7 A man is charged with murder.

8 There is a dispute over land.

9 Someone is caught fishing illegally.

10 A 14-year-old boy is charged with breaking a neighbour's window.

11 A woman has run away from her husband.

12 A teenage boy has stolen his father's truck.

Law and order

Today there is a lot of conflict between traditional law and order and the government's laws and the constitution.

Crime	Traditional law	Government law
Murder	Both sides pay compensation. Payback killing.	Criminal goes to court and is put in jail.
Stealing or lesser crime	Matter is dealt with by the village chief. Criminal stays in village and is given punishment at village level.	Criminal goes to district or village court. Might go to jail.
Minor disputes	Dealt with by village meetings and discussion.	Village court decides the punishment.

Respect for custom helps keep **law and order** where traditional values are still strong, especially in villages.

In the towns and cities, crime is more of a problem.

Many people cannot find work and have no money, so they turn to crime.

Many people do not trust the police because they can be very tough.

Because people do not trust the police, they do not cooperate with them.

Many people do not understand the new way of dealing with disputes. They are used to the old ways of payback, which, in their minds, is the way to balance things.

Find out about traditional ways of dealing with conflict in your area.

Find out what happens in your community when a crime is committed. Do the police deal with it or does the village chief?

Look carefully at the picture below and write seven sentences saying how the law is being broken.

 Read **Law in the Village**.

Traditional leadership

Traditional **big man** culture in the Highlands has ________________.

Leaders used to be older men who had earned the ________________ of their people.

They were good at making speeches and they kept the ________________.

At moka ceremonies, there was much ________________ and exchanges of food and pigs.

Old friendships were made ________________ and new friendships were made.

These big men wanted the best for the local people and helped to ________________ disputes.

Traditional leaders had resources that were used to look after their ________________.

respect	people
feasting	stronger
settle	peace
changed	

Talk to someone older in your community about traditional leadership in your area. How has it changed? Why has it changed?

 *Make a list of all the good things that came out of a moka ceremony.*

 *Write a description of a local leader who you respect. Say why you respect that person.*

 Read about Sir Michael Somare's story in **The Chief**. What made him a great leader?

Leadership today

Leaders today are usually much __________________ men.

Some of them use __________________ to become elected as ward councillors or village court magistrates.

Some of them have __________________ and this gives them power over the people.

In some Highland districts in PNG, the __________________ have become a time when these young leaders hold feasts to get people to __________________ for them.

elections	younger	guns
vote	bribery	

This feast is not like the **moka** ceremony. It is to show their wealth and to make people think that they are __________________.

People think that the free services they **provide** will continue after they have been __________________.

Many of these __________________ do not look after the people once they are elected.

They do not provide the basic goods and __________________ to the people.

They just want power and they use the __________________ for themselves.

generous
money
elected
services
leaders

Bribery is when people give you money, gifts or food so that you will vote for them.

Generous people give things to other people for free.

Provide means to give something that is needed.

For you to talk about

1. *Would you vote for someone just because he is rich?*
2. *Would you vote for someone you didn't know just because he made many promises?*
3. *Would you vote for someone because he had a gun and you were scared of him? A gun means violence. Is this a good thing?*
4. *Would you vote for someone who was a bully?*
5. *Would you vote for someone just because he looked important?*

What kind of person makes a good leader?

Talk about the qualities that a good leader should have.

 *Write a story about this.*

Choose some words from this list for your story.

honest	smart
fair	responsible
wise	good decision maker
truthful	positive attitude
strong	self-controlled
kind	

Use your dictionary to match the words from the box with their meanings below.

They do not get angry easily.

They have power.

They are very fair and care about others.

They spend their money wisely. They do not give money to their friends or spend it on themselves.

They make good judgments and solve problems well.

They always believe in good outcomes.

They always tell the truth.

They are clever.

They can be trusted to do the right thing.

They help everyone, not just some of the people.

They make good decisions about things.

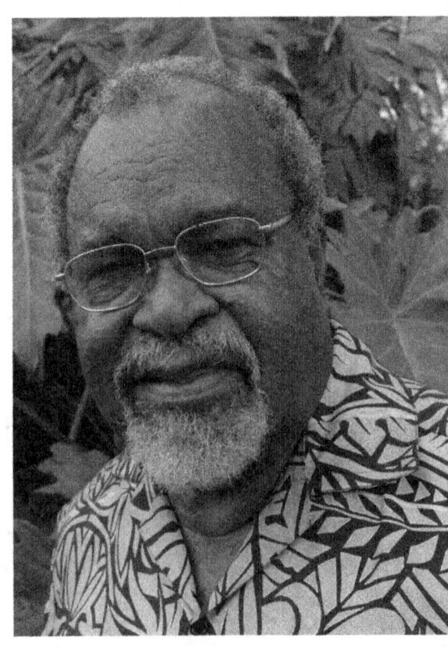

Sir Michael Somare

Some PNG leaders

Bill Skate

Lady Carol Kidu

Sir Paulius Matane

Find out about these PNG leaders. What things have they done for our country over the years?

Choose one of these leaders and write a biography about them like in The Chief.

Women in politics

Meri I Kirap Sapotim (MIKS) is a women's group that was started after the 2002 national election by women in the Highlands who had stood for local level government and national elections. These women felt that they had no chance to get elected as some of the men who stood for the elections bought votes through **bribery** and also used **violence** to get votes.

A Simbu woman said this after the election:

"Yupela ino ken ting ol meri kendidet long Simbu I bin lus long dispela election.

Mipela ino win tasol mipela ino lus. Long wanem? Ol man meri long ples, ol ino bin vot."

Violence means to threaten you or harm you or shoot you.

Bribery means that they paid people to vote for them.

 *Write down what she said in English.*

They want the people to be educated about things like:

- how to govern
- elections
- the use of guns
- bribery
- violence.

They want to see women in parliament as well as men, so that they can help run the country and make it a better place.

Discuss the roles of men and women in your community.

 *Write down a list of things that the women in your family do.*

 *If you are a girl, write a paragraph saying what you would like to do when you grow up.*

OR

 *Write about a woman that you know who is respected in your community. Say why she is respected.*

Some of the government's services

Here is a list of some of the government services in PNG.

- banks and financial services (looking after money)
- community and social services (looking after people's needs)
- engineering services (construction)
- business and tourism
- educational services
- health services
- communication services.

Draw up a table and use the above headings, then choose from the services below to go under the headings.

Waste management
Bank of PNG (BPNG)
Roads
Hospitals
National Tourism Office
University of PNG
Parks and gardens
Dump management
Health centres
Building projects
Institute of Business Studies
PNG Banking Corporation (PNGBC)
Post Courier
Chamber of Commerce
Primary schools
Nursing school
Botanical gardens
Tourism Promotion Authority

Wharves
Airports
High schools
National radio
Television
Pipelines
Ports
Bridges
Airstrips
Kindergartens
Post offices
Street lighting
Telikom PNG
PNG Power
University of Technology
Aid posts
National Library Service
The National

Air transport

International airports

PNG has international airports in Port Moresby, Lae and Tabubil.

Air Niugini flies to Sydney, Brisbane, Cairns, Honiara, Singapore and Manila.

It flies to other international airports like Hong Kong and Tokyo.

Find these places on a map of the world. Draw arrows to show where the flights go.

Local services

Air Niugini is the airline owned by the government.

There are regular flights to 20 main centres all around PNG.

It also has smaller planes that fly to over 100 airstrips around the country.

There are also missions and other companies that provide air services around PNG.

Finish these sentences:

1 An international airport means that ______________________________

____ .

2 PNG has three international airports. They are in ______________________

____ .

3 Air Nuigini flies to other countries. Some of these are ___________________

____ .

4 Air Niugini is owned by ______________________________ .

5 There are regular flights to ______________________ places in PNG.

6 Small planes fly to over ______________________ airstrips in PNG.

Sea transport

Because the roads are not that good and the planes are very expensive, many goods are shipped by sea.

International ports

A port is a place where ships can come into a safe harbour and tie up at a wharf to be loaded or unloaded by big cranes.

There are international ports at Port Moresby, Lae, Madang, Kimbe and Rabaul. Ships come to these ports from other countries bringing tourists and goods to our country.

Smaller coastal ports

There are smaller ports at Wewak, Kavieng, Oro Bay and Alotau.

These places have timber jetties where boats can tie up, but many of them have only beach landings. This means that boats have to be loaded and unloaded over the ship's side, into village boats or canoes.

There are passenger ships that run between Lae and the MOMASE (**Mo**robe, **Ma**dang and **Se**pik provinces) and New Guinea Island region.

There are also regular passenger runs between Bougainville and the New Guinea Islands.

Answer these questions.

1 *What is a port?*

2 *Name PNG's international ports.*

3 *Where are the smaller ports found in PNG?*

4 *How are they different to the international ports?*

5 *What does MOMASE mean?*

Roads

The main highways are:

- Hiritano Highway, which runs from Port Moresby through to Kerema
- The Okuk Highway (Highlands Highway), which runs from Lae through to Goroko, Mt Hagen and Madang
- Magi Highway, which runs from Port Moresby through to the Aroma coast.

There is no road connecting Port Moresby, the Highlands and the MOMASE region.

The best roads are in the towns.

Many roads need repairing and are only suitable for four-wheel-drive vehicles.

Most roads that join up to the main roads are not sealed.

In many remote places, traditional bush tracks are still the only roads available. Because these roads are rough, the trucks and vehicles that use them break down and wear out very quickly.

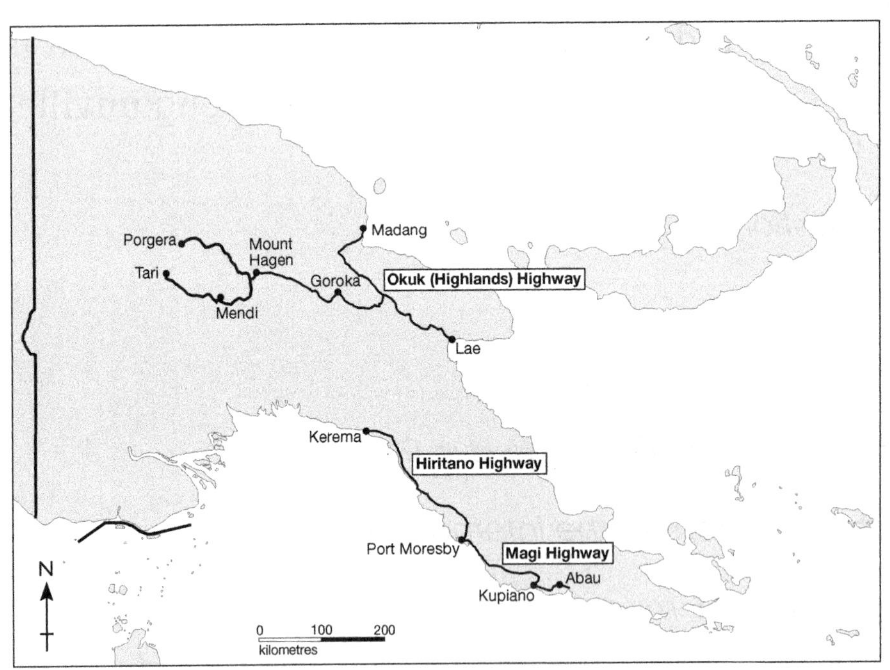

 *Copy this map of PNG showing the three main highways in PNG.*

Now draw in the international ports. Make up a symbol to show that they are ports.

Road building

Taim bipo: Road building and looking after roads in some parts of Papua New Guinea was done by the local village people.

The government gave them spades and picks. The people dug the roads out of the mountains.

Village elders decided that each family would be responsible for looking after a piece of the road.

This worked very well for many years.

Then the government started roading projects to help look after the roads by sending in machinery like bulldozers to grade the roads.

The government does not have enough money to grade all the roads in this country, so many local people still have to look after their own smaller roads.

Many people living along these project roads have been able to grow bigger gardens and make more money by taking their food along these roads to markets to sell them.

Women and children and people with only small amounts of money are able to get medical attention more easily. Children are able to travel to school by road.

It is now cheaper and quicker for these people to travel and easier for them to make money.

Where roads have been upgraded and sealed, there is also less erosion and flooding.

Write down the advantages of having roads looked after by the government.

Telecommunications

Telikom

Telephone and fax services (kwik piksa leta) are provided by a government-owned business called Telikom.

They can be used in most areas. Large towns have public telephones that are operated by phone cards or coins.

Radio stations

The National Broadcasting Commission **(NBC)** is a government-owned radio communication service that is received by all centres around the country. Some provinces have their own NBC radio station.

There are a number of commercial radio stations in Port Moresby and Lae.

Internet

Internet and email services are provided by private internet service providers (ISPs). Many people use this service to communicate with each other by email on their computers. This is a fast and easy way to communicate.

Postal services

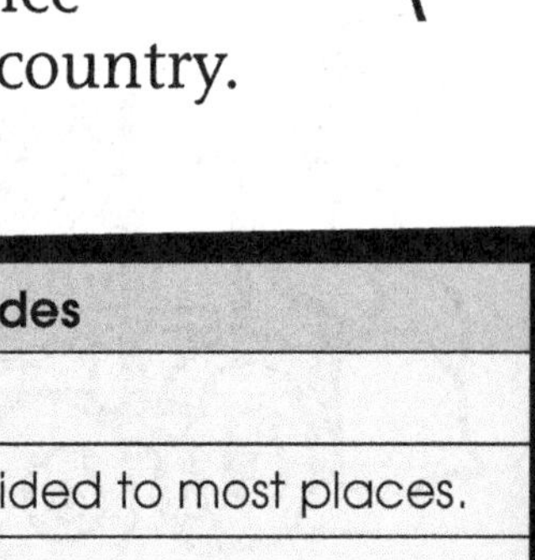

Postal services are provided by a government-owned business called **Post PNG**.

There are 36 post offices throughout the country. You can post letters and parcels here.

Post PNG also provides a same-day money transfer service called **Salim Moni Kwik** to 41 places throughout the country.

Copy this table into your book. Now fill in the table:

Name of service	Owned by:	Service it provides
Post PNG		
		Telephone and fax services provided to most places.
	Privately owned	
NBC		

Problems for the government

This is a speech made by the Prime Minister Sir Michael Somare in Mount Hagen on 3 September 2004.

We still have a long way to go in linking up our entire country through road, shipping and air transport services.

Once the government has improved things like roads, bridges and airports, it is now jointly the responsibility of the people and the authorities to make sure that these are looked after.

We must be able to have discussions, understanding and cooperation from everyone, so that we can all benefit.

This brings me to the issue of **good governance**.

To be able to do this, there must be good citizenship attitudes and responsible behaviour.

The government can repair these facilities, but if the community lets people **vandalise** and destroy them, then we are wasting our resources.

When we have to spend money to fix things, we have less money to use on other important things.

What does the government spend a lot of money on?

What do you think ***good governance*** *means?*

What does the community have to do to look after these facilities?

Pretend you are the Prime Minister. Make this speech to your friend in your own words.

Read **The Cassowary Chase**.

Vandals

Match the sentence beginnings with the endings.

Vandals are usually	**citizens.**
They destroy public facilities by	**windows.**
Sometimes they	**buildings.**
This is called	**for the damage they do.**
Sometimes they smash	**young people who are bored.**
Sometimes they break into	**damaging them.**
They are not good	**write all over walls and buildings.**
Everyone must pay	**graffiti.**

Robbery

Sometimes ________________ steal public property.

Things that are ________________ are often not replaced.

If wires are stolen out of a telephone or computer, then they ________________ be used.

If you see someone stealing something, you should call the ________________.

police thieves cannot stolen

Weather

Sometimes the weather can destroy man-made things (facilities) like **buildings**, **roads**, **bridges** and **airports**.

In the Western Highlands Province, three months of heavy torrential rains have caused floods in Dei District.
On 6 March 2006, the Avani Bridge between Kainantu and Goroka along the Highlands highway collapsed, stopping traffic between the Highlands and Morobe province.
There was no food and fuel and this made life very hard for the people in the local communities. (IFRC 22 March 2006)

1. *Which main facility was destroyed during the heavy rains?*
2. *Where was it?*
3. *What happened as a result?*

A long and heavy rainy season in Papua New Guinea has caused problems including homes destroyed by winds and flooding.
Still more dangerous has been a large number of landslides in the remote mountainous areas of the country, burying roads and cutting off villages that were already hard to get to. (IFRC 14 February 2006)

1. *How were the homes destroyed?*
2. *What is a landslide?*
3. *What damage was caused by landslides?*
4. *What happened as a result?*

Continuing heavy rains and unusual weather conditions in Papua New Guinea have been blamed for the latest damage to roads, bridges, homes and food gardens.
Main roads, bridges and beach hotels in the Morobe and Madang provinces are the latest to be affected by the king tides and flooding. (IFRC 30 August 2005)

1. *What things were damaged by the heavy rains?*
2. *What conditions did the heavy rains cause?*
3. *Find out what a **king tide** is.*

2 Learning about our Environment

Chapter summary

In this chapter you will:

✓ Learn how to read and draw a map
✓ Learn how to use a compass
✓ Learn about our mountains and rivers
✓ Learn about some volcanic eruptions in PNG
✓ Make a volcano that erupts
✓ Learn how to follow directions on a map
✓ Work out some codes
✓ Make a forest brochure
✓ Learn about insect life cycles
✓ Find out about endangered animals
✓ Learn how we can protect our animals
✓ Learn how animals can protect themselves
✓ Learn some interesting facts about PNG.

Cross-curriculum topics

These topics apply only to this chapter.

Topic: Community living

Strand: Community

Sub-strand: Places

5.1.4 Describe geographical features of the Province.

Topic: Environmental studies

Strand: What's in my environment?

Sub-strand: Plants and animals

5.1.1 Investigate and apply ways of using, protecting and conserving certain plants and animals.

Sub-strand: Links in the environment

5.1.3 Investigate the relationships between living and non-living things.

Topic: Science

Insect life cycle.
Endangered animals.
An insect pest in PNG.

Topic: Art

Symmetry: making butterflies.
Making a model volcano.
Making dice.

Topic: Drama

Perform the play 'Endangered Animals'.
Write a play about 'The Eruption.'

Maps

Maps of the world are found in a book called an atlas. Maps tell us where places and things are on a drawing. The drawing looks down on the country and sees it how a bird sees it, from high up in the sky (called a 'bird's eye view').

Some maps are **political maps**. This means that the map shows the boundaries or provinces made by the government. Can you find a political map in Chapter 1?

Another type of map is called a **physical map**. This map shows landmarks such as hills, mountains, airports and cities which are drawn in pictures or symbols on the map (see page 33).

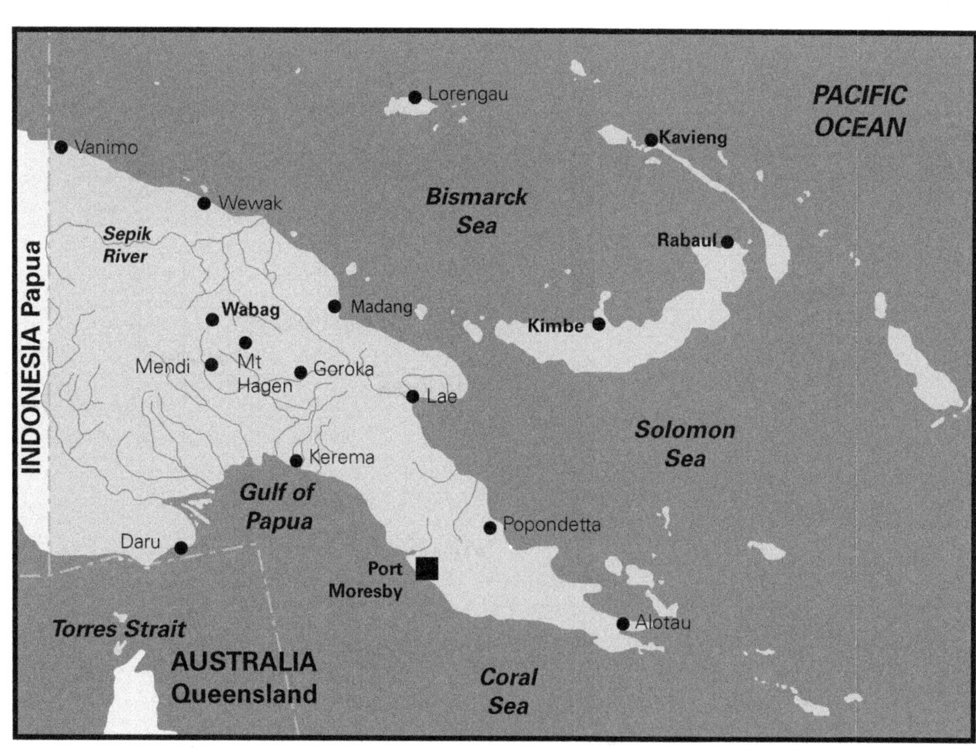

 *Copy this map into your book.*

Study a map to find out where these mountains are and draw them on your map. Write the names next to them in small letters.

Mt Kombiu	Mt Wilhelm	Mt Michael	Mt Yule
Mt Victoria	Mt Tuvurur	Mt Elimbari	Mt Bellamy

Find out where these rivers are and write their names on your map.

Sepik River	Purari River	Kikori River	Vanapa River
Fly River	Strickland River	Ramu River	

1 *Which is the highest mountain?*

2 *Which is the longest river?*

3 *What is the name of a river close to where you live?*

4 *What is the name of a mountain close to where you live?*

You may also find a **grid map** in an **atlas** (a book of maps). A grid is a table of squares. They are numbered so that it is easy to find a place. This is called a **grid reference**.

Study the map below.

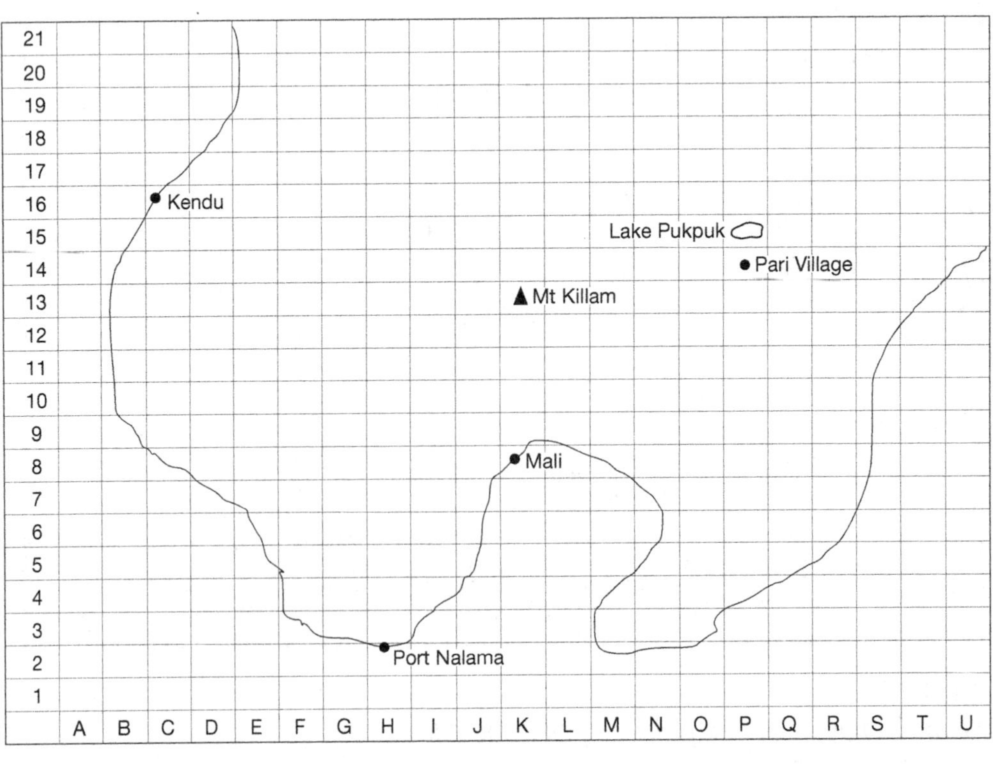

The grid reference for Mali is **K8**.

Find the grid references for: Lake Pukpuk, Pari Village, Kendu, Mt Killam, Port Nalama.

 *Make up your own grid and draw in some landmarks.*

Ask your friends to find grid references for them.

Maps use symbols to represent things. The symbols are explained at the bottom of the map in a box called a key. A key looks like this:

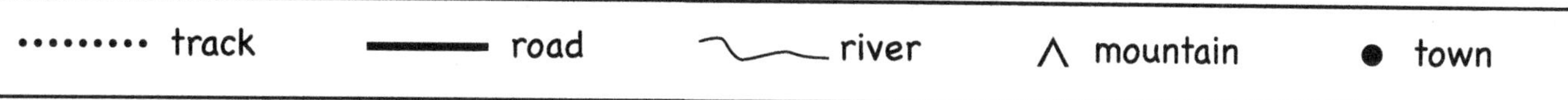

What do you think these symbols could represent?

Draw a physical map of your local area like this, showing landmarks, mountains, rivers, towns and villages, roads and any other main features. Make up your own key.

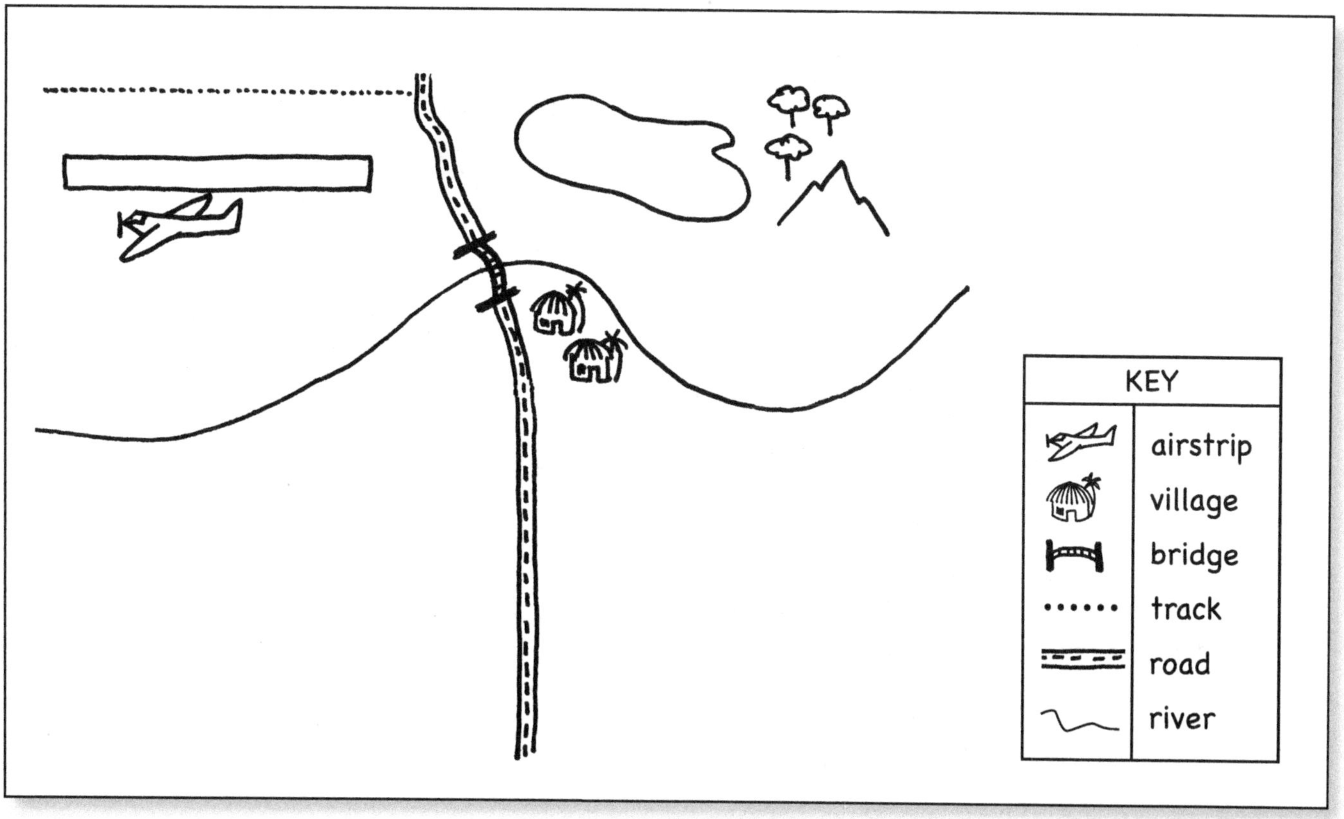

KEY	
	airstrip
	village
	bridge
	track
	road
	river

How people live on the Sepik River

Finish writing Kali's questions.

Who owns
____________________?
Our society is a paternal society. That means it's owned by men. My sister has no rights over the land. She is able to live here but she doesn't own the land.
Where
____
____________________?
What ________________
____________________?
My house is on the river bank. It is a semi-permanent house. The roof is made of iron and the walls are made of pungal from the coconut palm. It is made of bush materials. It gets very hot at my village but the house is cool.
What
____
____________________?
We grow cash crops like cocoa, coffee, vanilla and copra. We go fishing, but sago is our staple food. We eat rice, sago, beans, fish, and meat from cuscus and bandicoots. We buy lamb chops and beef in the town. We grow tomatoes, grains, beans and other local plants from the forest.

Volcanoes

Papua New Guinea has 14 **active** and 22 **dormant** volcanoes. All the active volcanoes have erupted at least once during the last 235 years.

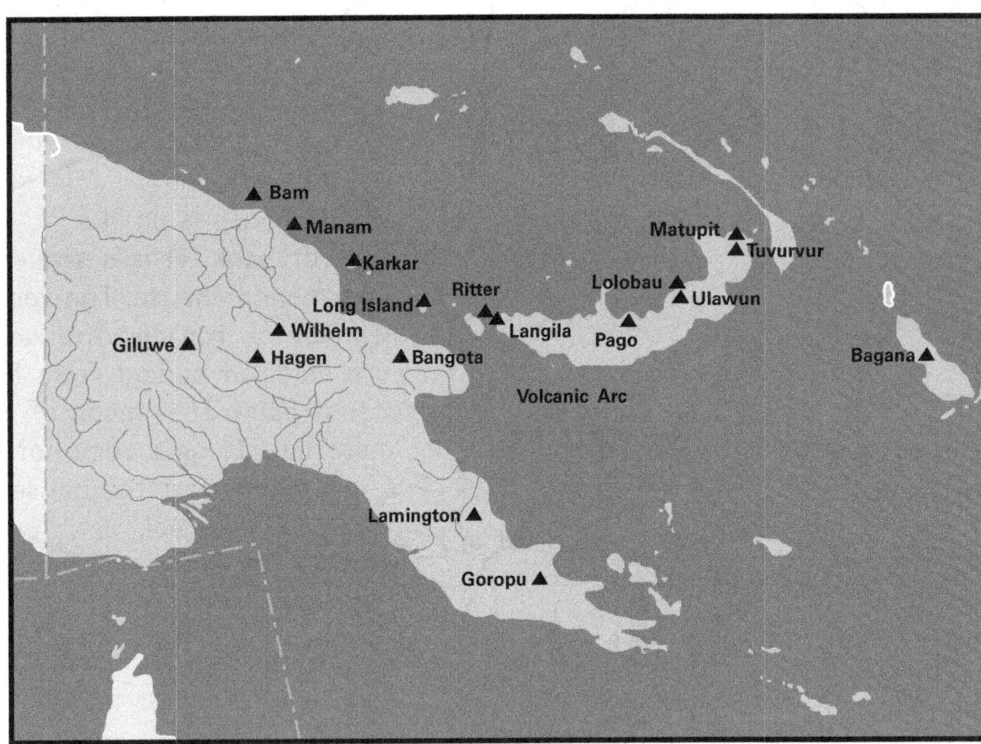

An **active** volcano can erupt at any time.

A **dormant** volcano is not active.

This map shows the volcanoes around the islands of PNG.

For you to do

 *Copy this map into your book and learn the names of the volcanoes.*

Find the mountain nearest to you.

How high is it?

Has it ever erupted? If so, when?

 *Draw a picture of it.*

Are there any stories that you know about this mountain?

Make up a legend about it.

Rabaul volcanic eruptions

Rabaul is built on an active volcano. There are a number of **dormant** and **active** volcanoes in Rabaul and the Tolai people who live near these have a saying:

"Tikana pakana takaum kilala na nilaun – una gire ra kaia na vuvuai."

("Once in your lifetime, you will experience a volcanic eruption.")

On 18 September 1994, an earthquake started shaking the Gazelle Peninsula.

At 6.00 a.m. on Monday, 19 September, **Tuvurvur** volcano began destroying Rabaul and the surrounding villages.

About an hour later on the other side of Simpson Harbour, another volcano, **Vulcan**, also erupted.

It buried many other villages on that side of the bay.

It destroyed the land, houses and gardens of many people living there.

Write a newspaper report saying what happened on 18 and 19 September 1994.

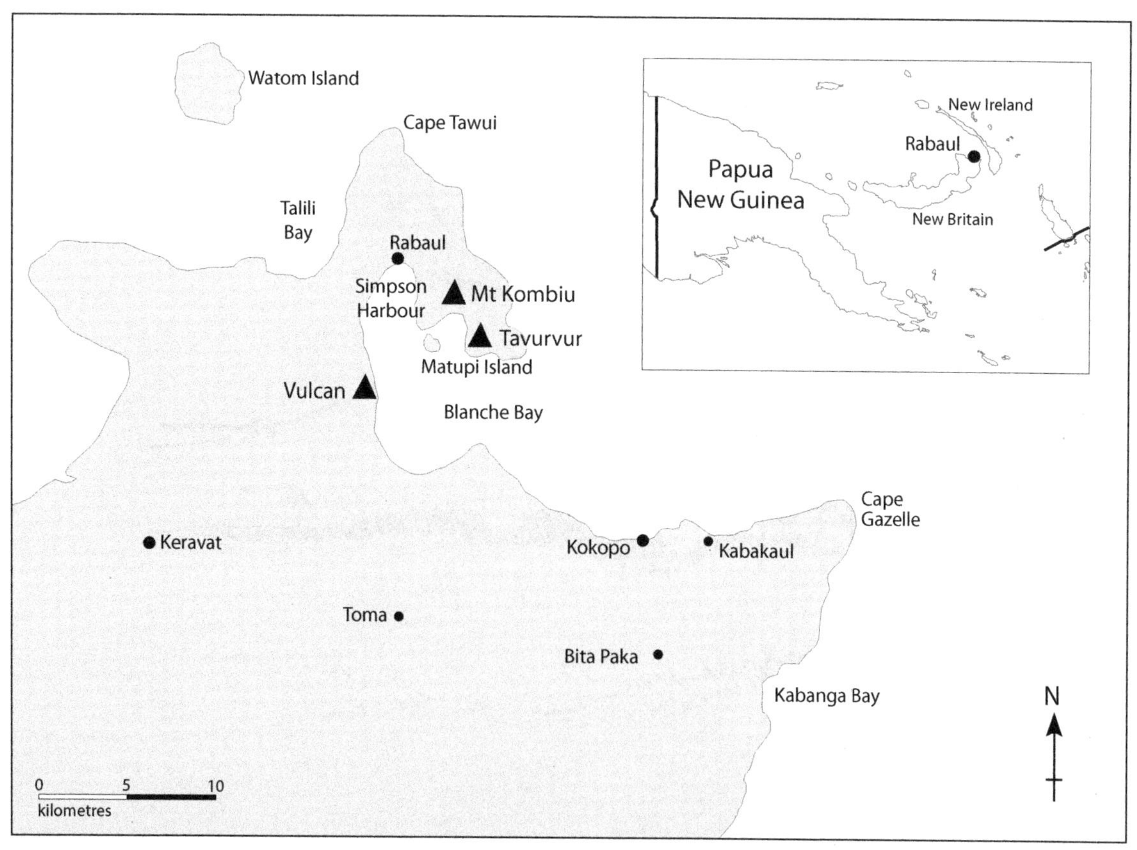

Mt Lamington

Can you find Mt Lamington on the volcano map on page 36?

Mt Lamington is 1600 metres high and about 150 kilometres to the north-east of Port Moresby.

In the middle of January 1951, Mt Lamington began to shake the earth.

The Orokaivan people who lived below it watched in fear as flames burst out of the volcano.

The dogs, pigs and birds knew what was happening and they all ran away.

Many local people kept on working, believing that the spirits would protect their houses and their gardens.

For almost a week, there were landslides, fireballs, shaking and red flames. Black smoke kept pouring out of the volcano.

Then on Sunday morning, 21 January, the whole side of the mountain blew out.

Hundreds of people died.

A dark cloud of grey ash rose high into the sky.

Red lava swept down the mountain and about 300 square kilometres of land were destroyed.

At midday, the area was as black as night.

The poisonous gas in the air killed many thousands of people.

Some people think that 4000 people were killed. Others think it was more like 12 000.

Answer these questions:

1. *Name six things that warned the people that the mountain was going to erupt.*
2. *Why did many local people stay in their houses instead of leaving?*
3. *What was the time and date of the eruption?*
4. *What killed the people?*
5. *What destroyed the land?*
6. *Work out how many years ago this happened.*
7. *Was it a good decision to stay in the villages after the warning signs?*
8. *Would you leave your home if a nearby volcano started to erupt?*

Match these words with their correct meanings:

fear	land that slides down a hill
protect	to throw out rocks, lava and ash
midday	hot liquid rock that comes down the side of a volcano when it erupts
lava	to look after
landslide	to be frightened
destroy	12 o'clock in the middle of the day
erupt	to ruin

Making a model volcano

Materials needed:

plastic bottle	cardboard	baking soda	tomato sauce or red paint
sticky tape	scissors	vinegar	

Method:

1 *Put some baking soda into a plastic bottle (about 4 teaspoons).*

2 *Make a cardboard volcano shape around the bottle and tape it in place.*

3 *Pour tomato sauce or red paint around the top of the volcano to look like lava.*

4 *Now pour vinegar into the top of the plastic bottle (crater) until the volcano erupts.*

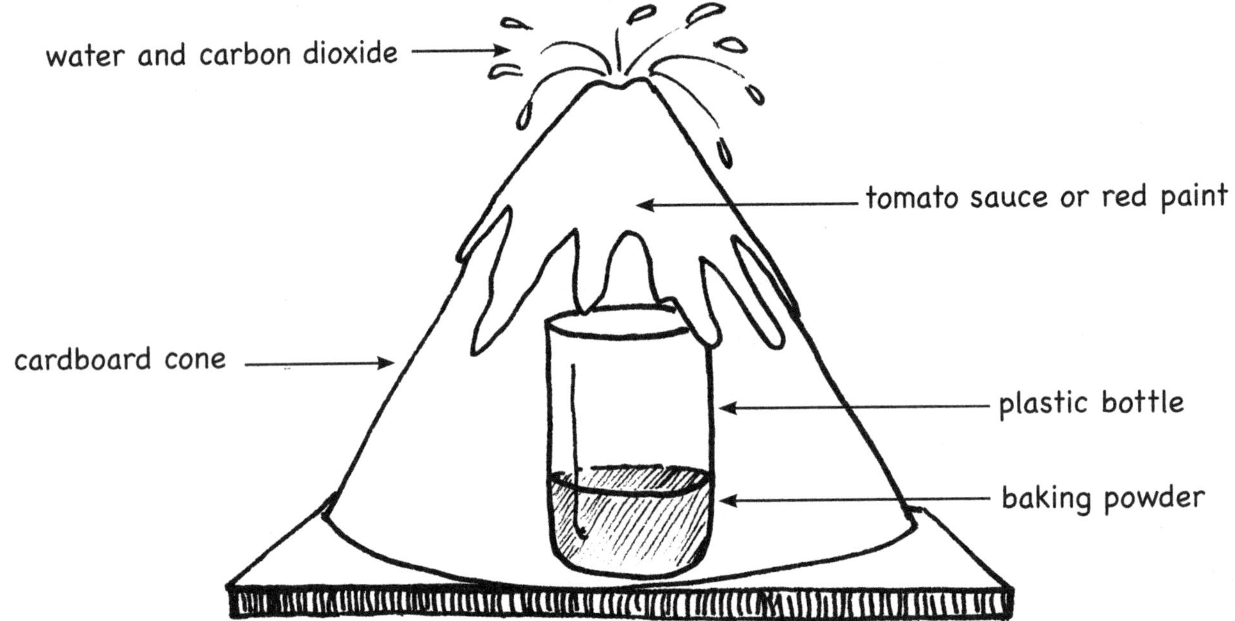

 *Make a model like this.*

 *Write a description saying how you made this volcano.*

What happened when you poured vinegar into the top of the plastic bottle?

Choose some of these words for your stories.

spurted	fizzed	exploded	trickled
lava	blew up	erupted	

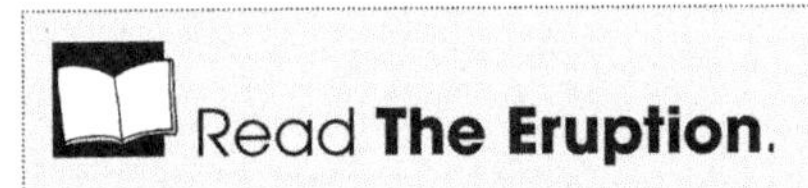

A compass

A compass is used to tell you which direction you are going in.

The needle of a compass is a small magnet that always points north and south.

The direction halfway between **north** and **east** is called **north-east**.

Draw a compass like this one in your book and learn the names of each direction. Can you work out what SE, SW, NW and NE mean?

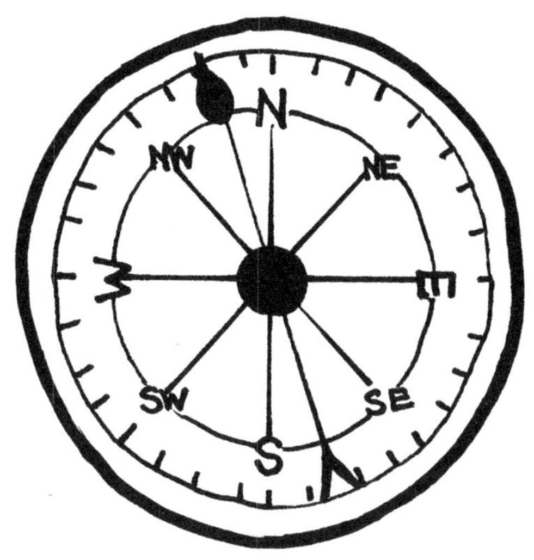

Make a compass

You will need:

a watch telling the correct time
a match.

Take off your watch and point the hour hand towards the sun.

Lay the top of the match halfway between the hour hand and the twelve, as in the picture below.

The match head will now point to the south and the other end will point north.

Try this outside at different times of the day to find north.

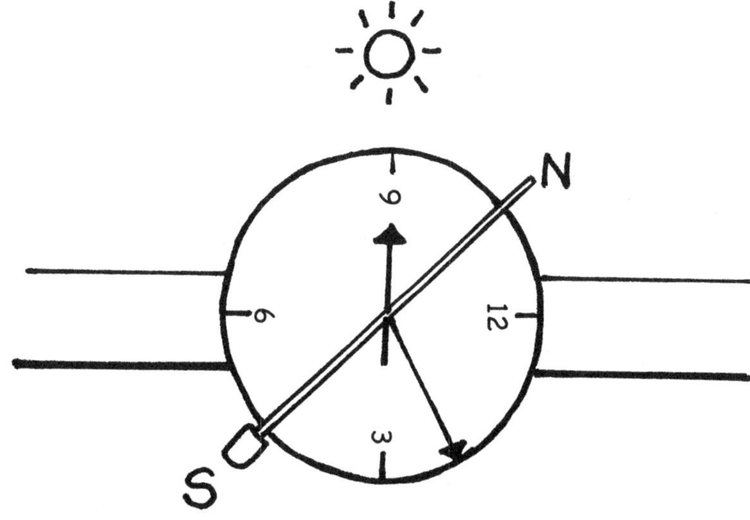

The Kokoda trail

Study this map.

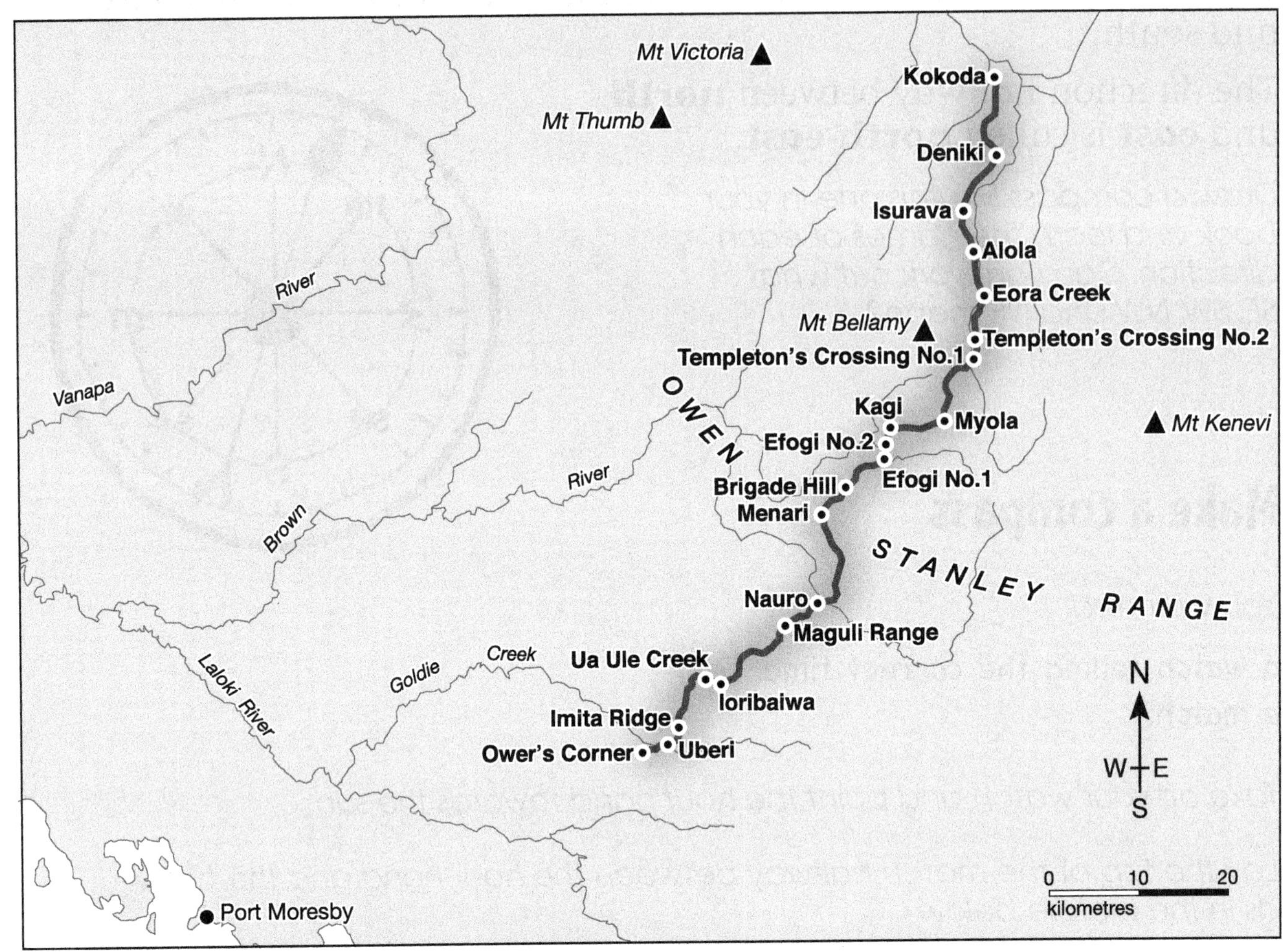

This map shows the Kokoda Trail.

It is an important track that was used in World War 2.

When the Japanese tried to come down through the Kokoda Trail to get to Port Moresby, the Australian and New Zealand soldiers fought them back.

Many of the PNG people who live along this trail helped these soldiers.

The double line at the bottom of the map is called a scale, to measure distances from 0 to 20 kms. Use a ruler or stick to measure these distances on the map.

Find the location of this area on the map on page 31.

Use the library or the internet to find out more about this trail.

Study the map on page 42 and answer these questions.

1 *How many villages are there between Owers' Corner and Kokoda?*

2 *What is the name of the main mountain range that runs through the Kokoda Trail?*

3 *Does the Vanapa River run through the trail?*

4 *What is the name of the mountain closest to the trail?*

5 *What is the nearest city to the Kokoda Trail?*

6 *About how many miles is it from Owers' Corner to Efogi No2 village?*

7 *A branch of what river runs through Nauro?*

8 *About how many kilometres is it from Templeton's crossing No1 to Kokoda?*

9 *About how many kilometres long is the Kokoda Trail?*

Using your compass

Look at the map on page 42 and find these directions.

1 *In which direction is Kokoda from Port Moresby?*

2 *In which direction is Kokoda from Myola?*

3 *In which direction is Mt Bellamy from Myola?*

4 *In which direction is Owers' Corner from Nauro?*

Study the map on page 31 and answer these questions.

1 *In which direction is Lae from Port Moresby?*

2 *In which direction is Kimbe from Madang?*

3 *In which direction is Lae from Popondetta?*

4 *In which direction is Goroka from Wewak?*

More compass work

Draw a table like this in your book.

Using your compass to give directions to draw this eagle. For each direction, move only one square. The first four have been done for you.

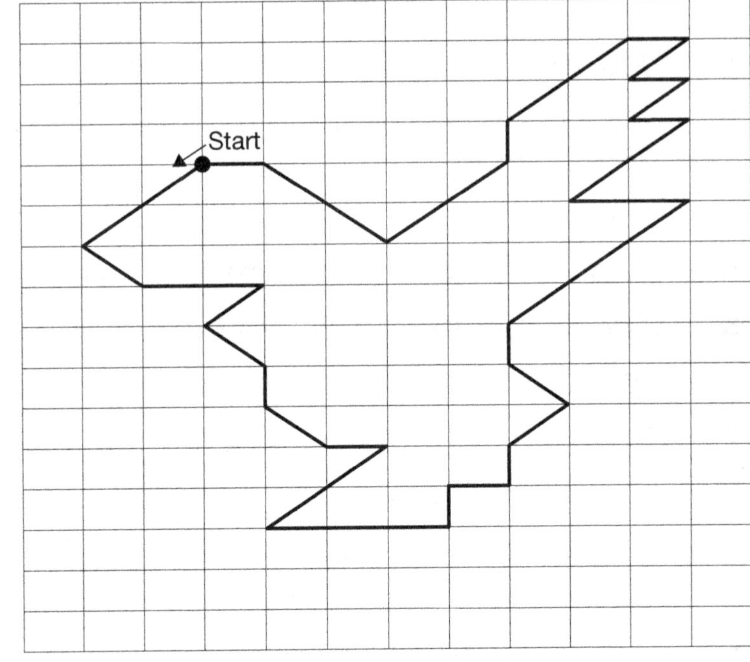

SW, SW, SE, E, ______________________

____

Draw this table into your book.

Follow the directions below to find something else in the bush.

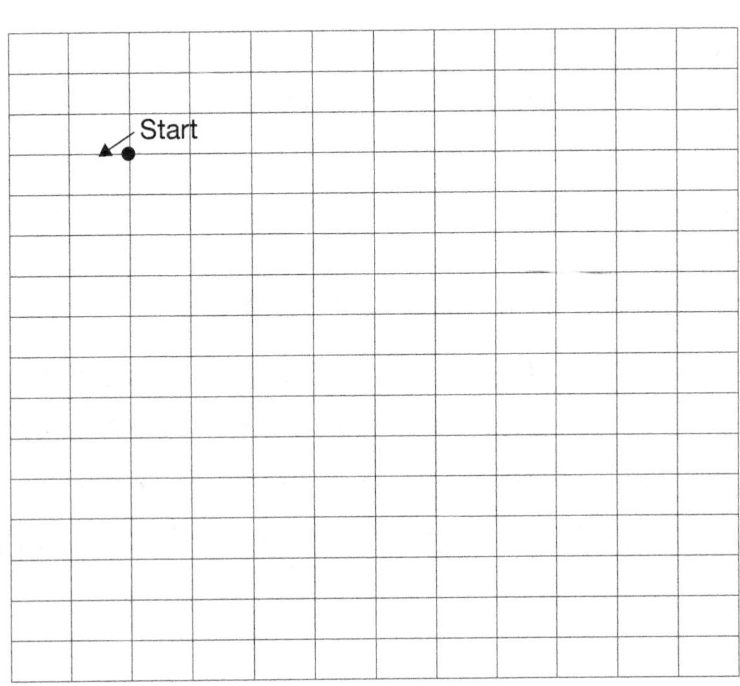

SW, SW, S, S, S, E, S, S, S, E, E, S, S, S, NE, NE, SE, NE, SE, SE, N, N, N, E, E, N, N, N, E, N, N, N, NW, NW, SW, SW, SW, NW, SW, NW, NW, NW.

Following directions

Pretend that Kali is on this map at X. He is lost and you must give him directions on the mobile phone to get to Popondetta.

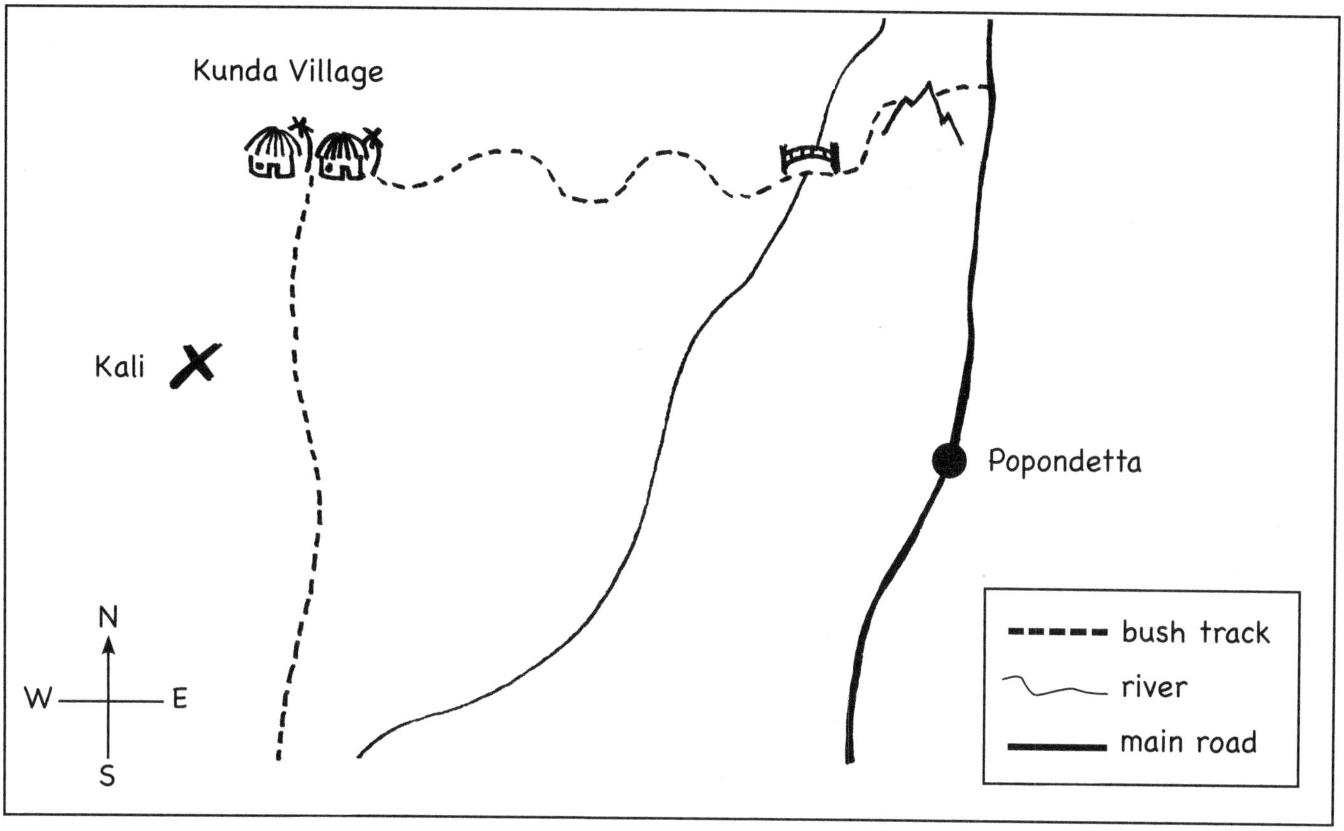

Kunda Village

Kali X

Popondetta

N
W E
S

bush track
river
main road

Using your compass, write down your directions like this:

Hello Kali! Listen carefully and I'll tell you how to get to Popondetta.

First you must walk __________ to find the bush track that leads to Kunda Village. Then walk __________ until you reach the village.

At the village turn to the __________ and follow the path to the bridge that crosses the river. Go over the bridge and take the track that goes ______________ behind the mountain. Follow it until you come to the main road. Go ___________ until you come to Popondetta.

Draw your own map and tell your friend where to go to reach a town or village, using a compass.

Codes

During the war, people used codes to send messages to each other by radio so that their enemies would not understand what they were saying.

Here are some easy codes for you to work out.

Code 897

A	B	C	D	E	F	G	H	I	J	K	L	M	N	O	P	Q	R	S	T	U	V	W	X	Y	Z
S	T	U	V	W	X	Y	Z	A	B	C	D	E	F	G	H	I	J	K	L	M	N	O	P	Q	R

Using the code above, work out what this message says. Write it in your book.

UGEW LG LZW HGGD VGOF TQ LZW NADDSYW SL EAVFAYZL SFV A OADD YANW QGM S EWKKSYW.

Make up your own code and write a message. Give it to your friend to work out.

Picture codes

Here is a letter written with picture clues instead of words. See if you can work out what it says.

Make up your own picture story and ask a friend to read it.

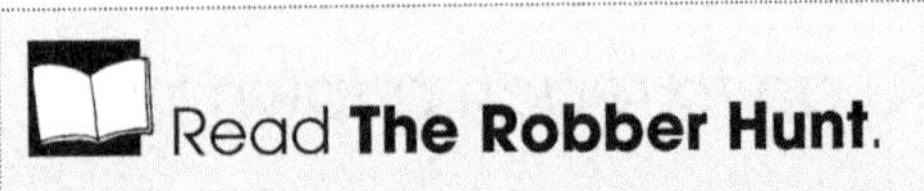

The Tufi fiords

A **fiord** is a long narrow stretch of sea between high cliffs.

Cape Nelson was made by the eruption of three volcanoes. The lava from these volcanoes made the fiords.

The fiords are sheltered and full of coral reefs and marine life.

The water in the fiords is 90 metres deep and the cliffs tower above up to 150 metres.

Mangroves grow out over the water's edge and waterfalls pour down into the sea.

The cliffs are covered in moss and beautiful orchids.

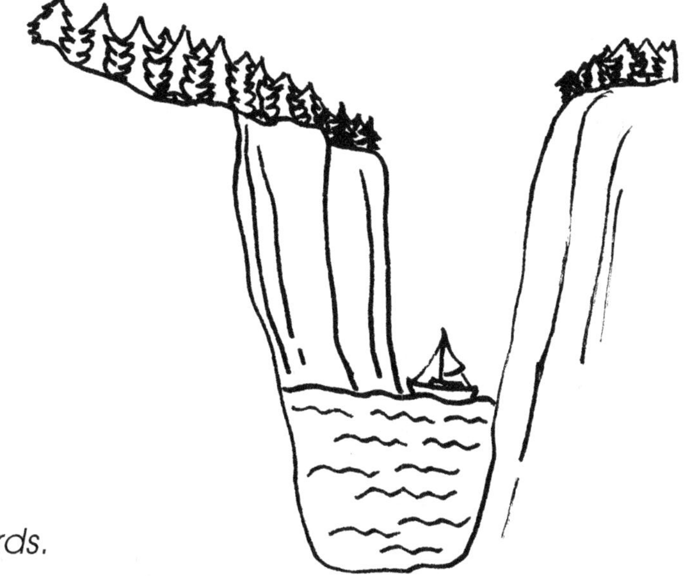

Describe the Tufi fiords in your own words.

For you to do: forest brochure

Is there a forest near your community? Design a brochure or small booklet for tourists. In it, tell about special places in the forest, such as a waterfall or swimming hole.

 *Draw pictures of some of the plants in the forest and name them.*

 *Draw pictures of some of the animals and birds in the forest and name them.*

 *Draw a map of the area and use dots …….. to show tracks or roads through the forest.*

Our precious forest

We invite you to visit our forest at ______________ . There are lots of well marked tracks in the forest for you to follow. You must not cut down any trees or harm any animals on your walk.

You will see orchids growing on many trees in the forest.

You will find lots of different types of mushrooms and fungus in the forest. You will also see Birds of Paradise and brightly coloured parrots in the forest.

Example of a forest brochure

Life cycles of insects

Insects are small animals that do not have a backbone.
All insects have a hard skeleton on the outside of their body.

Their body has these parts:

- head, thorax, and abdomen
- six legs
- two eyes
- two antennae.

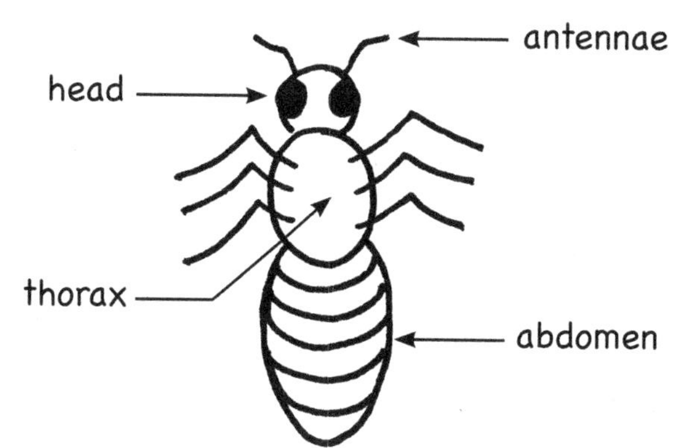

Mosquitoes

 *The life cycle of a mosquito looks like this. Copy it into your book.*

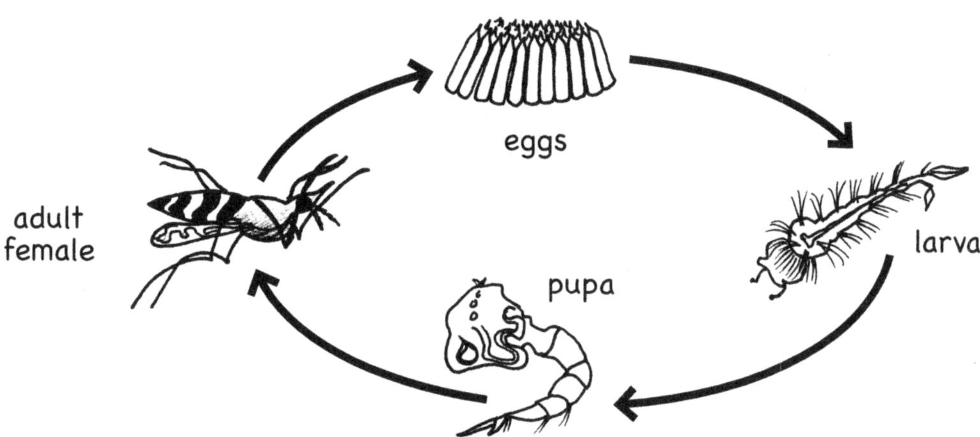

Mosquitoes lay their **eggs** in water. It might be in a small container or in the swamp.

The **larva** lives in the water.

It feeds on tiny living things in the water.

The **pupa** does not eat but is very active.

The **adult** comes out of the pupa case.

Go outside and search for mosquito larvae in water. Pour some kerosene on the water to kill the larvae.

Butterflies

The butterfly starts as an **egg**.
It hatches into a **caterpillar.**
Then it becomes a **pupa**.
Finally it emerges as a fully grown **adult**.

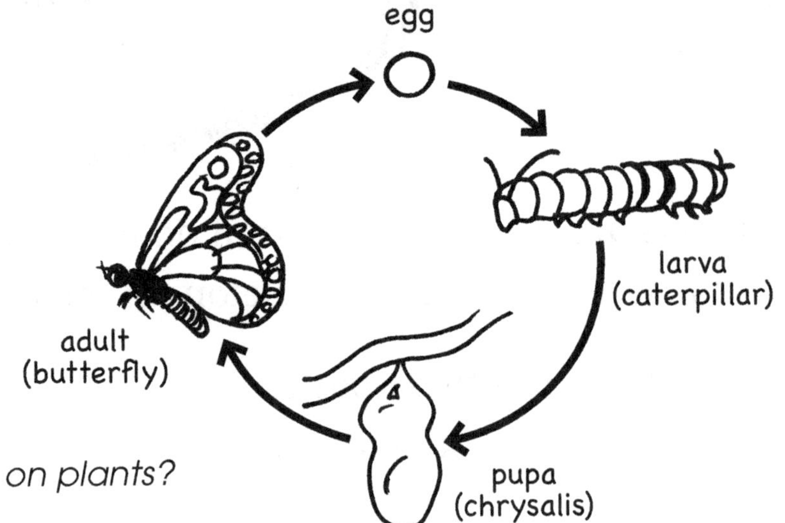

Can you find any of these outside on plants?

Draw them.

Ants

Copy these pictures of the life cycle of an ant into your book, putting them in the right order.

larva

egg

adult

pupa

Symmetry

Butterflies are symmetrical.
This means that if you cut it in half, one side is the same as the other.

Study these pictures.

butterfly

moth

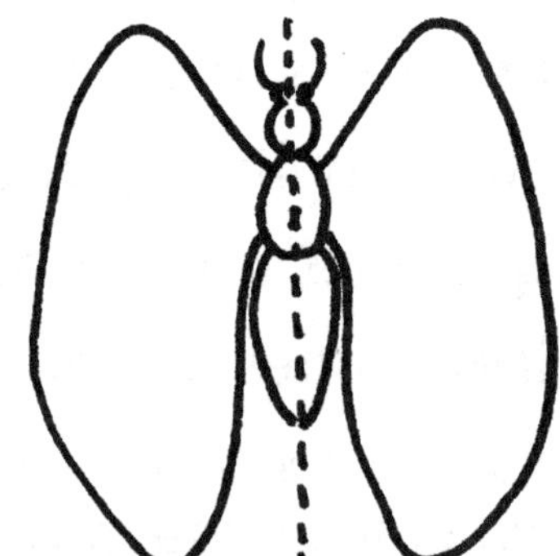

Draw one of these butterflies or moths and colour it in.

Read **The Butterfly Farm**.

An insect pest

Two of the biggest problems with many of our resources are pests and disease (sickness).

Pests can eat our cash crops.

Disease can kill our plants and animals.

Pests are living things that harm other living things.

Banana skipper butterfly

The larvae of these butterflies strip the leaves from banana palms.

This slows down the ripening of the fruit and makes the bananas much smaller.

It spread quickly through PNG in 1983 and destroyed 60 per cent of the leaves on the trees in some areas.

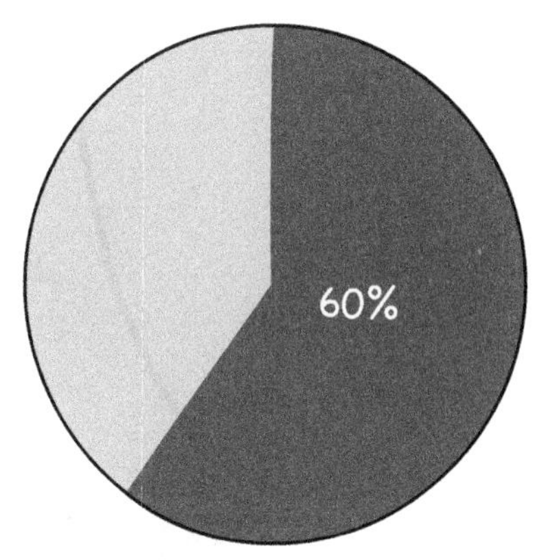

Scientists found a wasp that eats the banana skipper butterfly.

The wasp now keeps the butterfly under control.

1 *Why is the banana skipper butterfly a pest?*

2 *What damage did it do in 1983?*

3 *How was this pest controlled?*

Game: spider gets the fly

How to play: *Make a small spider out of cardboard. Make a dice.*

The game is played by two players. The first player throws the dice and moves that many spaces anticlockwise around the web.

The next player does the same. You must move your spider down to the next level of the web to find the next number.

***To reach the fly**, the winner must throw the correct number to land on the fly in the centre. (33)*

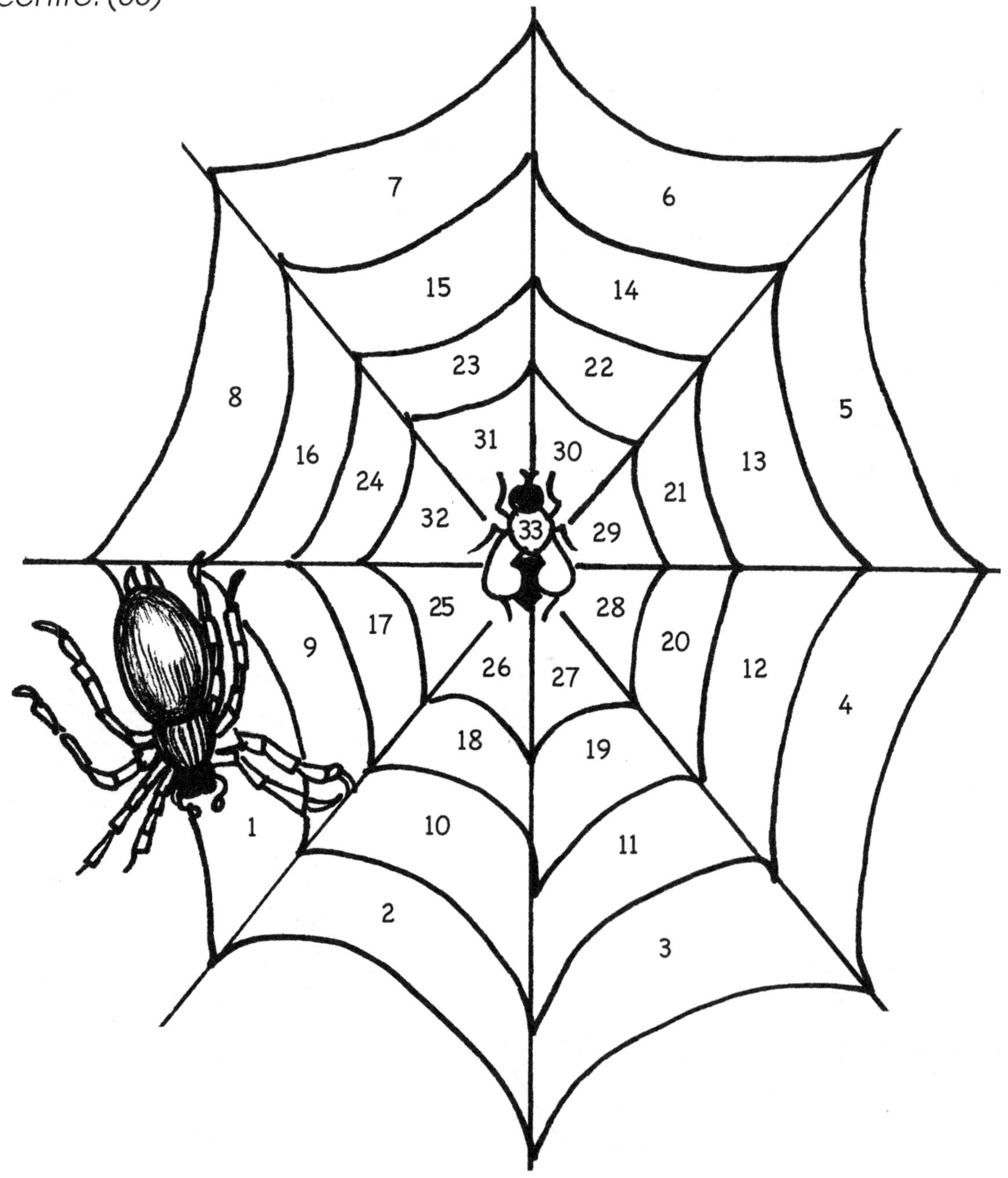

Endangered animals

Read the play **Endangered Animals** and complete the sentences below.

1 People hunt turtles for their ________________, their ________________ and their ________________.

2 People hunt birds of paradise for their ________________.

3 People hunt dugong for their ________________.

4 People hunt lizards for their ________________ to make ________________.

5 People hunt cuscus for their ________________ and their ________________.

6 People kill birdwing butterflies to ________________ them.

Endangered means that there are not many left.

Extinct means that there are none left.

Protected means that no one is allowed to kill them.

Find out which of these animals are protected in your community. Draw them.

dugong

turtle

cassowary

cuscus

tree kangaroo

bird of paradise

Making good decisions about protecting animals

In PNG, people have traditionally managed their environment wisely.

In Manus, there are community laws to protect the green turtles and dugong (sea-cow). No one is allowed to kill them as there are not many left. They are allowed to breed and live unharmed so they do not become **extinct**.

We have already talked about how many communities stop their people from over-fishing the reefs to allow the fish to multiply.

The government has made national parks and wildlife management areas to protect native animals and their habitats (homes) and plants.

Can you find out where the national parks are?

Find out if there is a wildlife management area in your province. Draw it on a map.

Many national animals are protected by the government. It is against the law to kill some of them unless they are caught by local people with traditional weapons for traditional purposes.

 *Write a story about how some animals in your community are protected.*

How animals protect themselves

Some animals protect themselves with camouflage. This means that they look the same as the place where they live, so they can't be seen easily.

Can you find eight insects or animals in this picture that are camouflaged?

Sometimes they use special parts of their bodies to protect themselves.

Study the pictures below. Can you match the body part with the animal underneath?

Write a sentence about each creature, saying how it uses its special body part to protect itself.

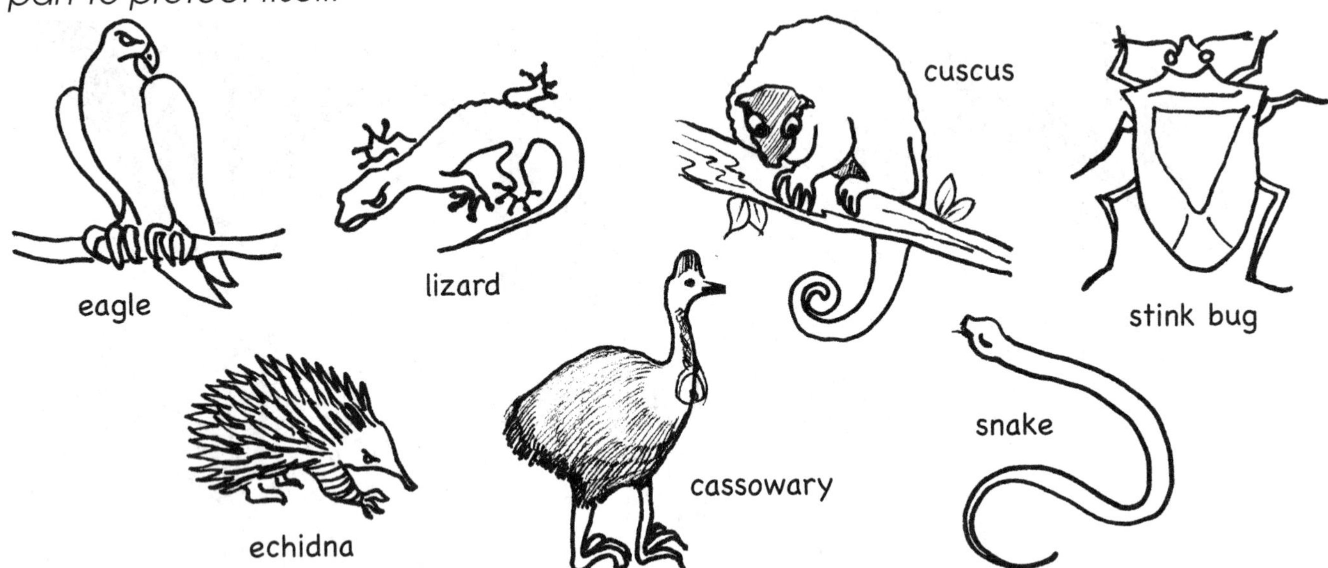

Look at these pictures and write a sentence about how these animals protect themselves.

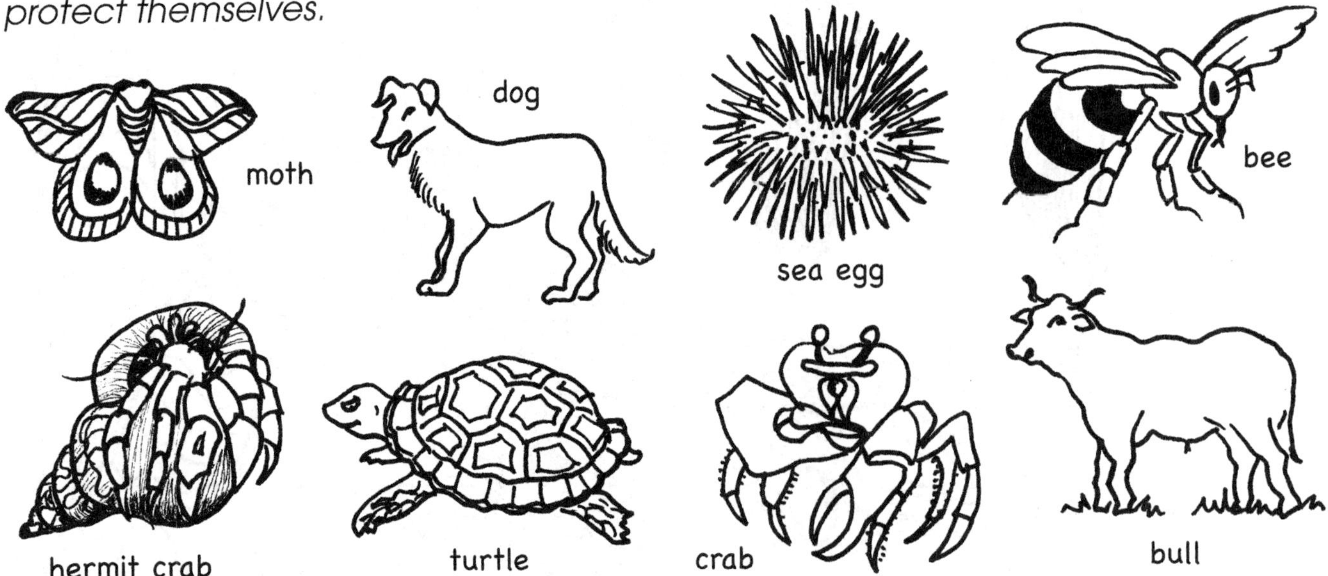

Can you think of any more examples?

Interesting facts about PNG

New Guinea "contains more strange and new and beautiful natural objects than any other part of the globe [world]."
(Sir Alfred Russell Wallace)

Here are some interesting facts about our country. PNG has:

- more types of orchid (a type of bush flower) than anywhere else on earth
- more types of mangroves than anywhere else
- almost all of the world's birds of paradise and tree kangaroos
- the world's largest pigeon, smallest parrot and longest lizard
- one-fifth of the world's languages
- the world's third-largest tropical rainforest
- some of the richest and largest coral reefs in the world
- as much plant and bird species as Australia in one-tenth of the land area.

orchids

parrots

mangroves

Draw some plants and birds in your area.

3 Making Good Decisions about our Resources

Chapter summary

In this chapter you will:

- ✓ Learn about logging in PNG
- ✓ Learn about facts and opinions
- ✓ Learn about logging safely
- ✓ Make decisions about fishing in PNG
- ✓ Study some animals and fish
- ✓ Play a fish game
- ✓ Learn more about food chains and food webs
- ✓ Find out how we get water to our houses
- ✓ Learn about the water cycle
- ✓ Do a water cycle experiment.

Cross-curriculum topics

These topics apply only to this chapter.

Topic: Environmental studies

Strand: What's in my environment?

Sub-strand: Plants and animals

5.1.1 Investigate and apply ways of using, protecting and conserving certain plants and animals.

Sub-strand: Changes in my environment

5.1.2 Investigate consequences of major changes and make informed decisions to conserve environment.

Sub-strand: Links in the environment

5.1.3 Investigate the relationships between living and non-living things.

Strand: Managing resources

5.2.1 Design and apply good practices to sustain the environment.

Topic: Health

5.2.2 Assess unsafe situations in the community to reduce harm and promote health.

Make sure water resources are clean.

Topic: Art

Making a reef box diorama.

Making birds: origami.

Making bird cards.

Topic: Science

Water experiment.

Topic: Game

Fish game.

String game (food chain).

Pesticide game.

Making good decisions about logging

A **good decision** is when you work out the best thing to do about something.

Everyone is very excited.

Dad stops them.

Just a minute means 'wait and think about it!'

Write all the speech bubbles above and on page 59 in sentences using speech marks to say who is speaking.

Facts and opinions

Amo and Dad decided to get more information (**facts**).

Can you think of some other things that they need to find out?

Finish writing Dad's questions.

What is your opinion about this?

Would you like to have lots of money? Why?

What could be some of the bad effects?

They found out these facts:

- The logging company may destroy a lot of the forest.
- A lot of chemicals and mud could go into the river.
- Many trucks could go past the village.
- The people would suddenly have a lot of money to spend.

A different point of view

Pretend you are Dad and write an argument ***against*** *logging.*

Now pretend to be Angon and write an argument ***for*** *logging.*

Discuss and write a report about a major development in your area. What are the effects of this development on your community?

After finding out about all the facts, Amo called another meeting.

This is what the men say:

This is what the women say:

Here is what Amo says about the logging company in Tok Pisin.

"Samting gutpela bilong ol dispela kampani bai stap liklik taim; samting nogut bai stap longpela taim."

 *Can you write down what Amo said in English and Tok Ples?*

 *Write down what you say about this problem.*

Before logging

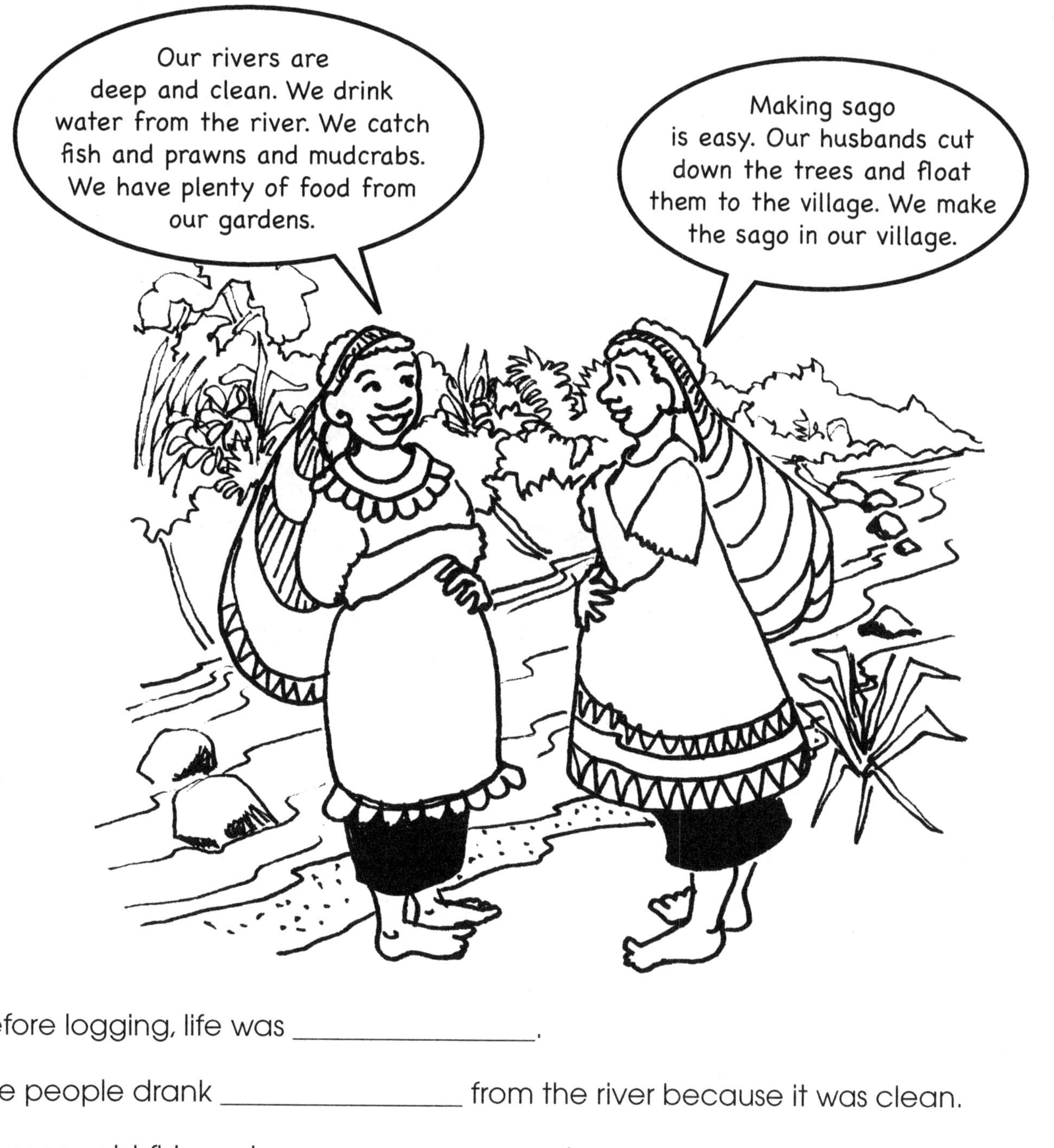

Before logging, life was ________________.

The people drank ________________ from the river because it was clean.

They caught fish and ________________ and ________________.

They got plenty of food from their ________________.

Making sago was easy because ____.

Read **Making Birds**.

After logging

Now the rivers are dirty. They are shallow and full of mud. If we drink the water we get sick. Our canoes get stuck and the fish are dying. There are floods and our gardens are no good.

The men cannot float the sago trees to the village now. We have to stay in the bush for many weeks to make sago.

After _______________, life was hard.

The people cannot drink the water from the river because it is _______________.

Now there are not many _______________ to catch.

The _______________ are flooded and now there is no food.

Sago making is not easy now because _______________.

What are the good things about logging?

What are the bad things about logging?

 *Write down your opinion.*

What are people doing about the problems with logging?

Rangers are being trained to go out and speak to the people in other districts to help them to look after the forests and not cut down all the trees. They tell them not to let logging companies cut down all their trees.

Eco-timber: Logging safely

There are lots of trees in our forest and Dad thinks that we can cut down some of them ourselves to make some money.

With this sawmill, we can cut the timber ourselves.

Is it hard to use?

No. But we must learn how to use it safely and learn how to look after it!

Put speech marks in the sentences below.

1 If we buy this portable sawmill, we can cut down the trees ourselves, said Dad.

2 Will it damage the forest? asked Amo.

3 No! said Dad. We will cut down only a few trees, then move it to a different place.

4 If we buy it, we can make money for the village, said Peta.

Write down what you think are the advantages and disadvantages of using a portable sawmill.

Making good decisions about fishing

A **ban** means that it is not allowed.

A ban is made on nets less than 2.5 inches.

Punishment:

- A fine of K50 to be paid within one month.
- Net taken away and returned when fine is paid.
- If the fine is not paid, the offender will be taken to the village court.

A ban is made on poison rope fishing.

Punishment:

- A fine of K100 to be paid within two weeks.
- If the fine is not paid, the matter will go to the Fisheries Management Committee.

A ban is made on dynamite fishing.

Punishment:

- A fine of K100 to be paid within two weeks.
- If the fine is not paid, the matter will go to the Provincial Fisheries Office.

A ban is made on dumping rubbish in the sea.

Punishment:

- A fine of K10 to be paid within two weeks.
- If the fine is not paid, the matter will go to the village court and the offender will do one day of community service as well as paying the fine.

 *Write down how each of these rules is protecting our fish.*

Make up a rule to stop people putting bleach into the water. What is a good punishment for someone who does this?

Make a list of all the things in the picture above that are destroying fishing.

Read **Riwo Fish Legend**.

Dynamite fishing

It takes many, many years for coral and reefs to be made, but in one blast, dynamite can completely destroy the reef and all the marine life living in it.

Reefs are also destroyed by homemade bombs. The fishermen get World War 2 bombs lying around Port Moresby, take out the gunpowder and make their own bombs with it.

The **Fisheries Act** was a law passed by the Government in 1994 to stop dynamite fishing in PNG. This law was passed not only to protect fish but also to protect the lives of people. However, many people still break this law and use dynamite and homemade bombs for fishing.

Read this newspaper article.

> **Central Province**
> 1 January 1996
>
> A young man from Tatana was killed on New Year's Eve while welcoming in the New Year.
> He and some friends made the bomb from some dynamite that they got from a blasting site near Port Moresby.
> Another youth was also injured in the blast and has lost a hand.
> Several people have been killed by dynamite over the past few years because they have not been aware of the danger.

Answer these questions:

1 *What law was passed to ban dynamite fishing? When was it passed?*

2 *What damage does dynamite fishing do?*

3 *Why is dynamite fishing also dangerous to people?*

4 *What two main places do people get the dynamite from?*

What is your opinion about fishing with dynamite?

Protecting turtles

In Lababia Village, many older people remember seeing many more turtles when they were children. Some remember seeing as many as twenty or thirty turtles a night on the beaches when it was nesting season.

Now, they only see one to six a night.

Since 2004, Lababia Village, the Village Development Trust (VDT), the PNG Office of Environment and Conservation and the South Pacific Regional Environment Program (SPREP) have all helped to protect the leatherback turtles in PNG.

The community has set aside its land as a wildlife preserve area (Kamiali Wildlife Reserve) and the villagers are involved in looking after the leatherback turtles that nest on their beach. They tag and count the turtles each night and also protect the turtle eggs that are laid along a part of the beach.

There is a real danger that these turtles will become extinct if we:

1 ________________ the turtle eggs at the market to get money.

2 ________________ the turtles accidentally when fishing.

3 ________________ the beaches where turtles lay their eggs.

4 ________________ turtles to eat.

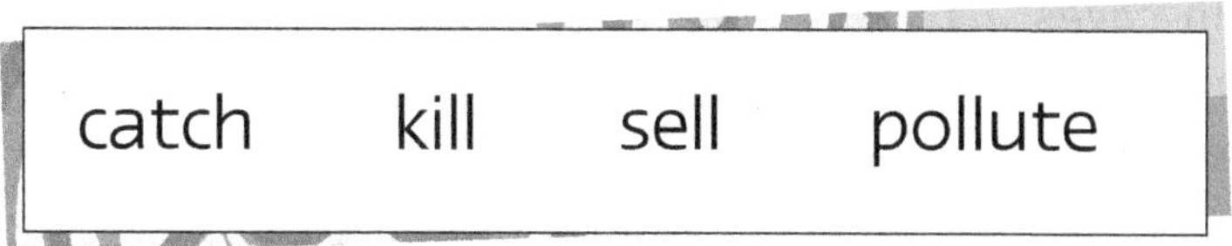

catch kill sell pollute

Why are plastic bags dangerous to turtles?

Talk about other ways you can protect birds and animals in your environment.

Weird happenings

Sharks have been seen swimming along the sea wall at Buruni's lower village during very high tides.

They have also been seen under the houses at Hanuabada village.

Baruni fishermen who were using flashlights for night diving said they were chased by huge sea snakes while diving on the reefs near Motukea.

Some women who were collecting crabs in the mangroves have said that they saw a large number of sea snakes east of Motukea.

People believe that dynamiting and excavating have helped to make these things happen.

The people of Baruni believe that the supernatural world has been polluted. The Koitabu people believe the 'Tabu', the supernatural beings that own the land and live in caves or hollow parts of trees, can change into any living form and scare people for having done bad things to their secret places.

Write about the weird things that are happening near Motukea.

Sea cucumbers

Talk about why a missing species upsets the food chain.

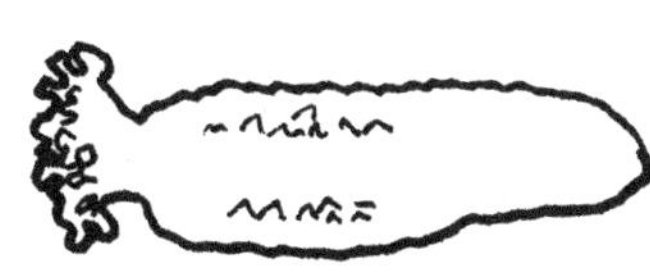

Why do you think the price is higher today?

Which of these things are more important?

Getting good money for a short time	Personal safety	Conservation	Preserving the food chain	Selling our resources overseas

Food chains

All living things depend on one another to survive.

A food chain consists of organisms that depend on each other as food.

A food web is made up of many food chains within a natural community of all the organisms in an area.

Many animals eat more than one thing and each link is important to the entire food web system.

Food chains are made up of four main parts.

1 The sun provides **energy** for all living things.

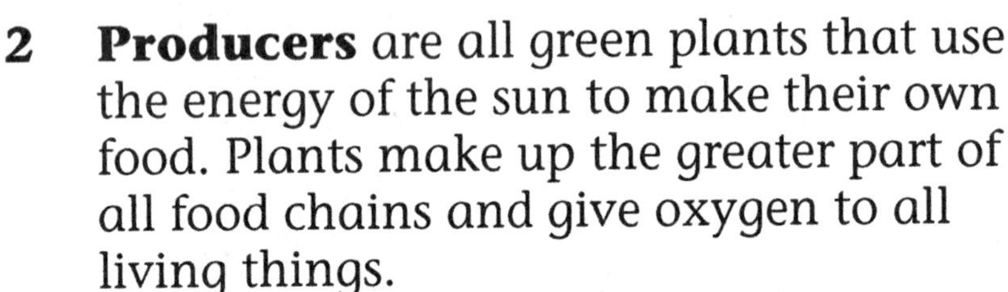

2 **Producers** are all green plants that use the energy of the sun to make their own food. Plants make up the greater part of all food chains and give oxygen to all living things.

3 **Consumers** (eaters)

(a) Carnivores (meat eaters)

Can you think of another carnivore?

(b) Omnivores (meat and plant eaters)

Can you think of another omnivore?

(c) Herbivores (plant eaters)

Can you think of another herbivore?

(d) Parasites (living off other organisms)

Can you think of another parasite?

(e) Scavengers (animals living off dead animals)

Can you think of another scavenger?

4 **Decomposers** like bacteria and fungi change dead matter into nutrients. Gases are put back into the air, water and earth.

nitrogen
carbon

An example:

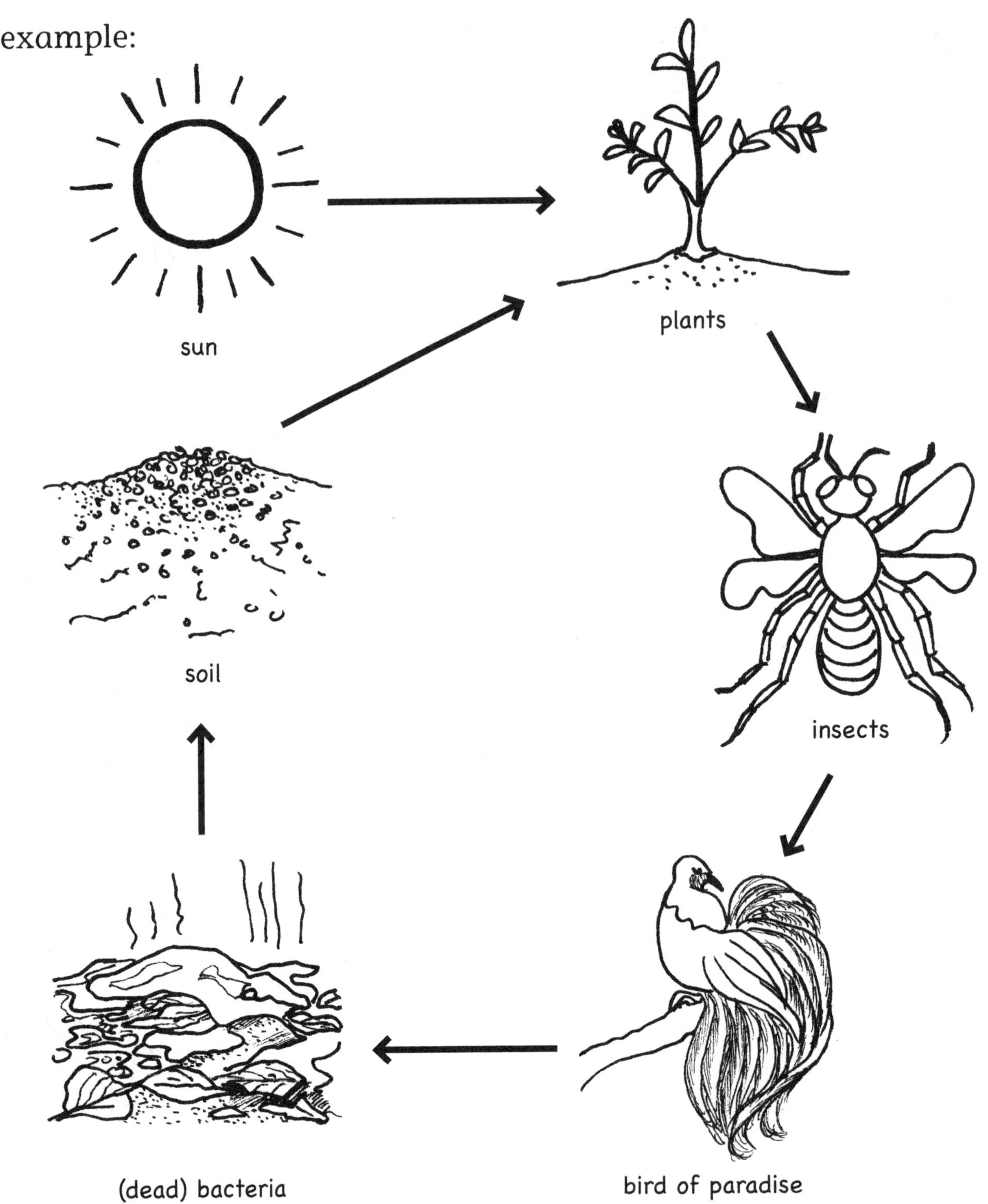

The sun gives energy to the plants. The plants are food for the insects (flowers, fruit, leaves, bark). The insects are eaten by the bird of paradise. The bird of paradise dies and **decomposes** into dead matter or bacteria. This turns into soil which gives energy back to the plants along with the sun.

Rule up a table like this in your book. Sort these into the right columns:

tree	sheep	mushroom	bat
horse	tick	bird	cuscus
grass	seagull	sun	crocodile
mosquito	tree kangaroo	plant	frog
goat	flea	fungi	
rat	fly	cat	
dog	person	snake	

Decomposers	
Scavengers	
Parasites	
Herbivores	
Omnivores	
Carnivores	
Producers	
Energy	

Life in the food chain

Look at the pictures below and sort them into the correct order that they would happen.

Write them in order in your book.

Owls and eagles eat snakes, small animals, small birds and bigger fish.

Using the sun as energy, plants like grass and weeds grow in the stream.

Sunlight gives the stream light and warmth for things to grow in.

Insects and shrimps eat the plants growing in the stream.

Small fish, frogs and small birds eat insects and shrimps in the stream.

Small animals, snakes and bigger fish eat the small fish, frogs and small birds.

Imbalance in the food chain

The food chain is finely balanced. When one link is taken away, or a new link added, an **imbalance** occurs and disaster can follow.

In the 1930s, moths were damaging crops of kaukau in the Gazelle Peninsula and the people were going hungry. There was nothing in the food chain in this area that ate the moths.

So, in 1936, cane toads from Queensland were brought into the Gazelle Peninsula to eat the moths. There are now many of them in the lowlands. They live in grassy areas, in towns and villages and also in rainforests. They eat many types of small animals, including Papuan black whip snakes.

Answer these questions:

1. *What was damaging the kaukau crops?*
2. *Where was this happening?*
3. *When was this happening?*
4. *What happened in 1936?*
5. *Where do the cane toads live today?*
6. *What else do they eat?*

In the 1960s, a pond weed (salvinia molesta) from South America was accidentally put into the Sepik River.

Because it was not part of the natural habitat, there was nothing in the food chain that ate it. It grew so quickly that it soon blocked all the rivers and lakes. Canoes could no longer travel on the waterways and the fish died from lack of oxygen. The people who relied on fish to eat starved.

Finally, the plant's natural enemy in Brazil was found. It was a small weevil (bug). Many weevils were put into the river, and after five years the weevil kept the weed under control.

The talapia and carp survived and people were able to catch the fish again.

Answer these questions:

1 *Which country did the pond weed come from?*

2 *How do you think it could accidentally be put in the river?*

3 *Why did it grow so quickly?*

4 *What two things happened because of this weed?*

5 *What happened to the people living beside the river?*

6 *What was found in Brazil?*

7 *What did the weevils eat?*

8 *How long did it take for the weevils to get the weed under control?*

9 *What type of fish lived in the river?*

10 *In which PNG river did this happen?*

Copy this grid into your book.

Find the names of the PNG animals on the grid.

If they eat only plants (herbivores), colour them green.

If they eat only meat (carnivores), colour them red.

If they eat both plants and insects (omnivores), colour them yellow.

S	T	R	E	E	K	A	N	G	A	R	O	O	B
N	M	P	T	U	R	T	L	E	W	A	K	V	A
A	C	R	O	C	O	D	I	L	E	T	U	R	T
K	G	E	C	K	O	N	S	C	U	S	C	U	S
E	C	A	S	S	O	W	A	R	Y	B	L	D	M

These bats eat insects. They are important to people because they eat a lot of mosquitoes which give us diseases.

What would happen to us if all the bats died?

Look at the table that you completed on page 75.

Starting with the sun and the producers, make a food web using some of the animals on your table.

sun → grass → plants → trees

When too many shells, corals and sponges are taken from the reef, this can cause an **imbalance in the food chain** on the coral reef.

A good example of this is the 'crown of thorns' starfish. It is now destroying some reefs.

Scientists think that this is caused by overfishing of the starfish's main food, which is the trochus shell. Because there were not enough trochus shellfish for the starfish to eat, it has started to eat coral.

The enemy of the starfish, the triton shellfish (conch shell), has also been overfished. This means there will be more starfish destroying the coral.

Explain this diagram to a friend, in your own words.

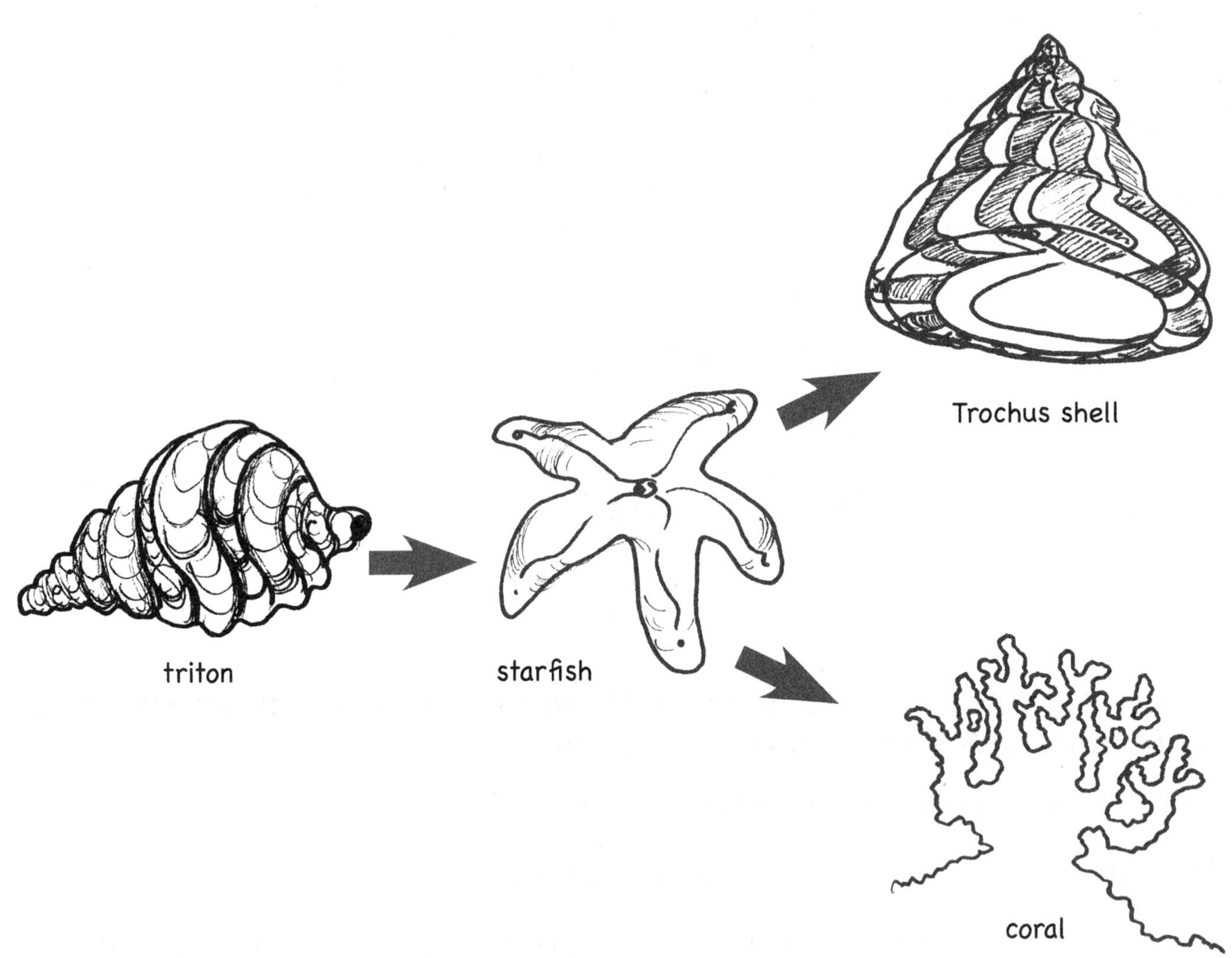

Traditional or introduced

Sort these things into two columns, traditional and introduced.

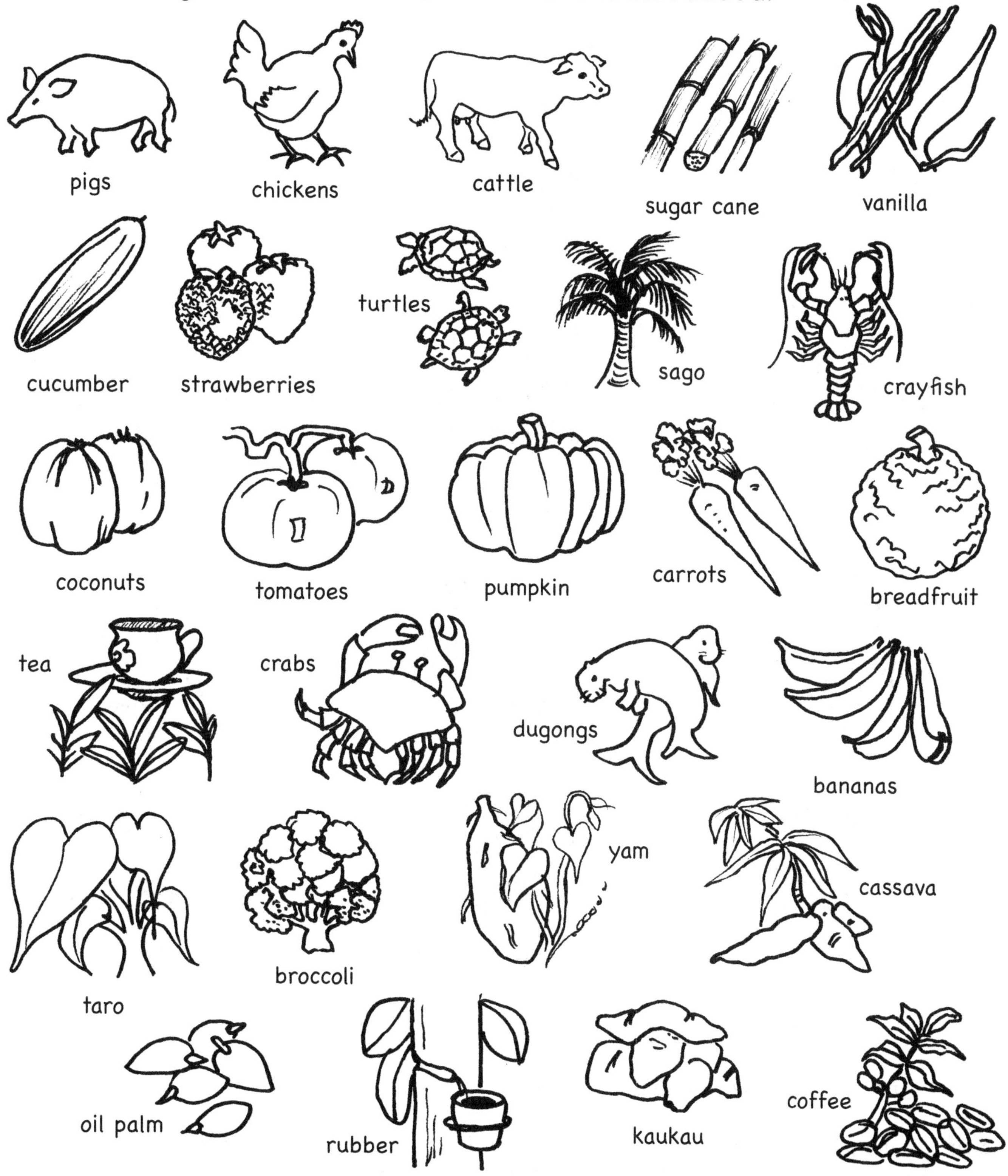

pigs

chickens

cattle

sugar cane

vanilla

cucumber

strawberries

turtles

sago

crayfish

coconuts

tomatoes

pumpkin

carrots

breadfruit

tea

crabs

dugongs

bananas

taro

broccoli

yam

cassava

oil palm

rubber

kaukau

coffee

Animals of Papua New Guinea

These animals are found in Papua New Guinea.

crocodile

sugar glider

cassowary

tree kangaroo

cuscus

bat

owl

gecko

hawk

taipan

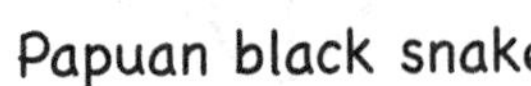

Papuan black snake

cane toad

 *Copy these pictures into your book and learn their English names.*

 *Put them into alphabetical order.*

 *Pretend that you are one of these animals. Write a story about your life and how you hunt for food. Who hunts you?*

Food webs

Most animals are part of more than one food chain and eat more than one kind of food to get energy. These **interconnected** food chains form a food web just as a spider's web is interconnected.

Fill in the time when you think the animal hunts for food: day or night.

Animal	Time the animal hunts	Food	Where it's found
crocodile		fish, small animals, birds	rivers, swamps
sugar glider		sap, nectar, bugs, baby birds	lowland forests
cassowary		fruit, berries, insects, small animals	
tree kangaroo		fruit, vegetation	trees in the Highlands
bat		fruit, insects	coastal
cuscus		fruit and leaves	all areas
owl		insects, small animals, snakes	all areas
gecko		insects	all areas
hawk		small animals, birds, rats	all areas
taipan (snake)		bandicoots, rats, small birds, bats	Central Province lowlands
Papuan black snake		frogs, bats, insects, geckos	sago swamp or coastal rivers.
cane toad		small animals, Papuan black snakes, geckos	grassy areas in lowlands

Interconnected means to join up.

Making a food web

This is an example of how some of the food web interconnects.

Look at the chart on page 83 and see if you can make your own food web using the things on the chart.

To make the web you must ask: What eats this? (Or what does this give energy to?)

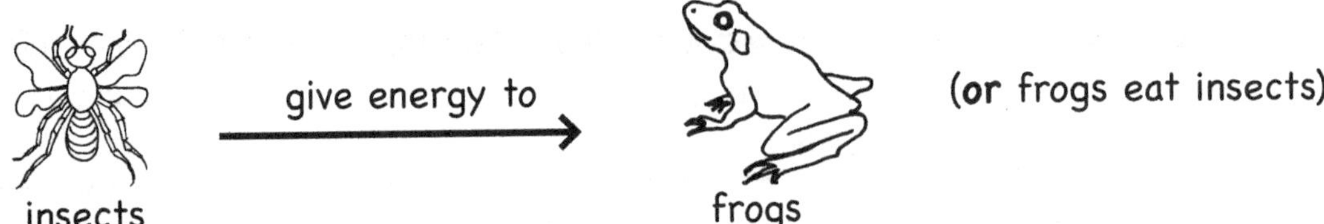

Study this chart and then make your own without looking at this diagram. To start, copy the things on the top line into your books.

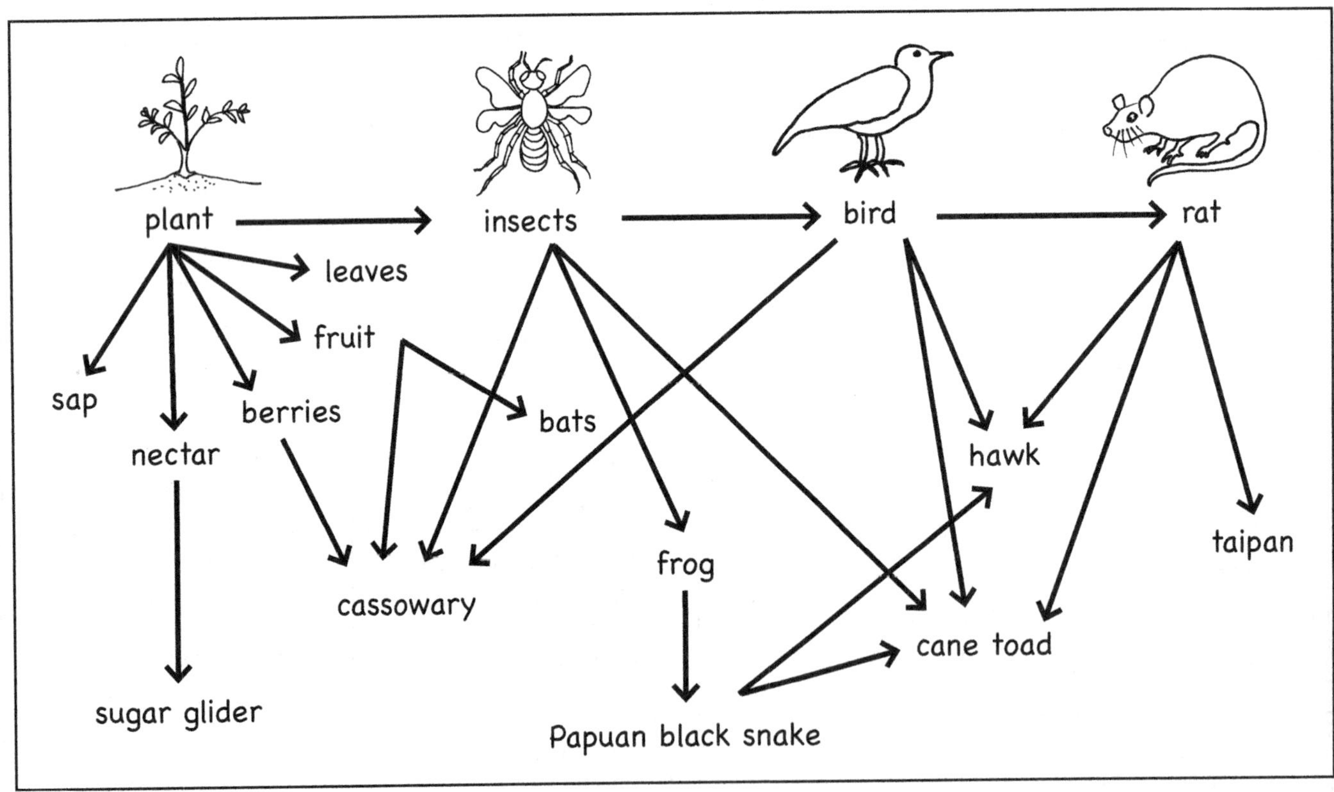

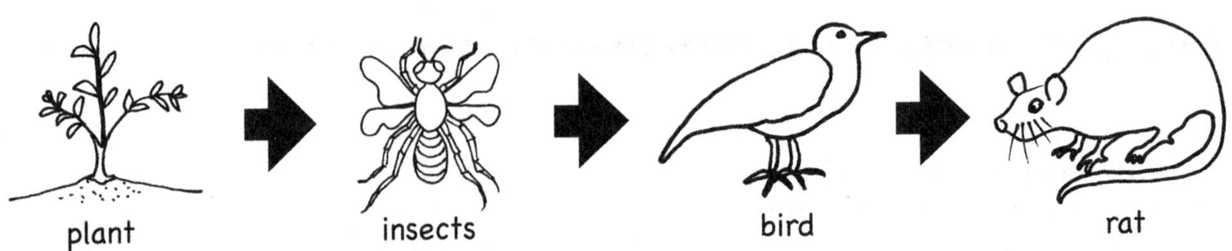

Coral reef food web

Look at the pictures below.

Piscivores (fish eaters)

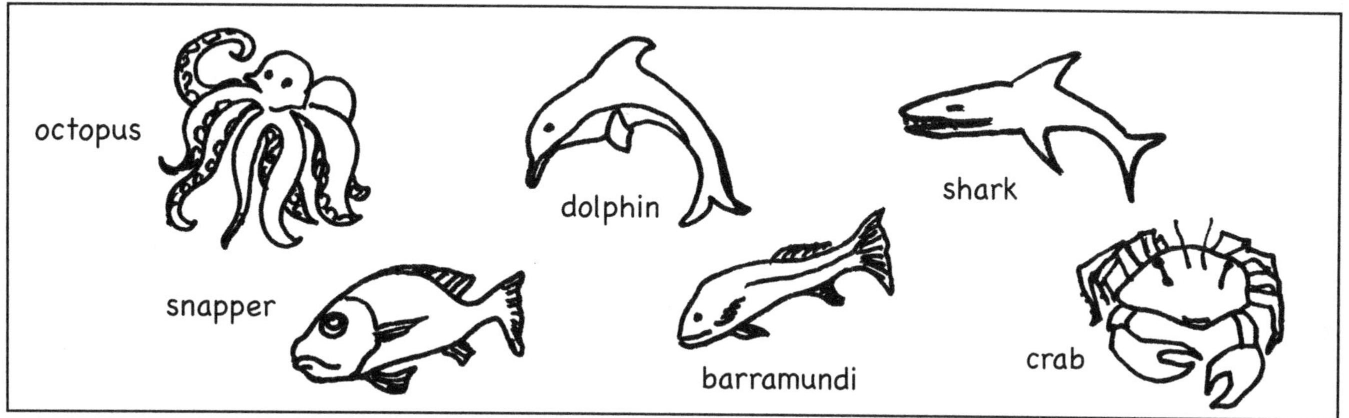

Omnivores

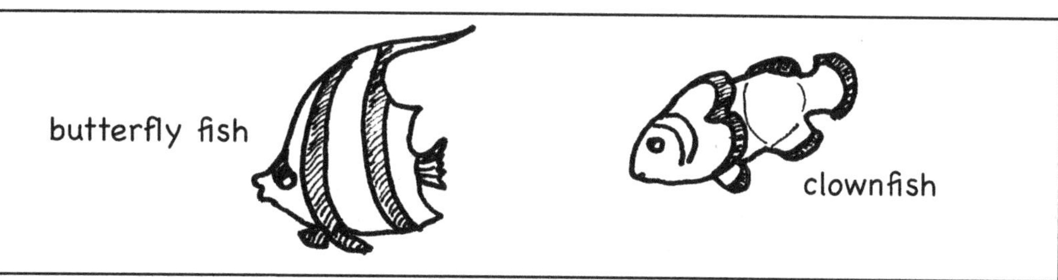

Herbivores

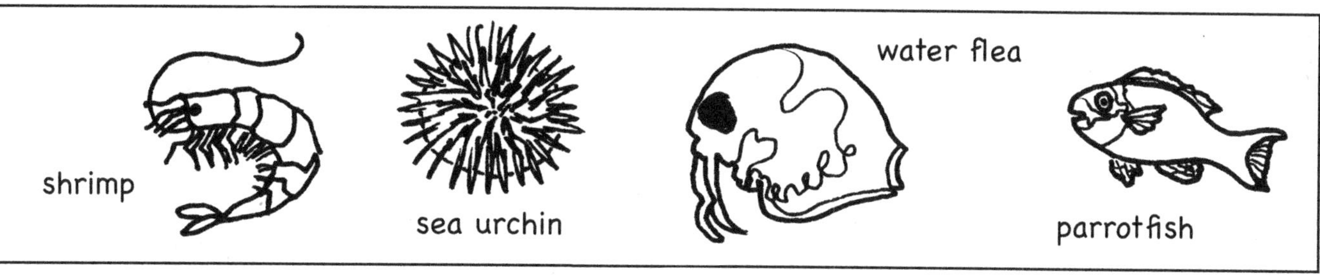

Producers

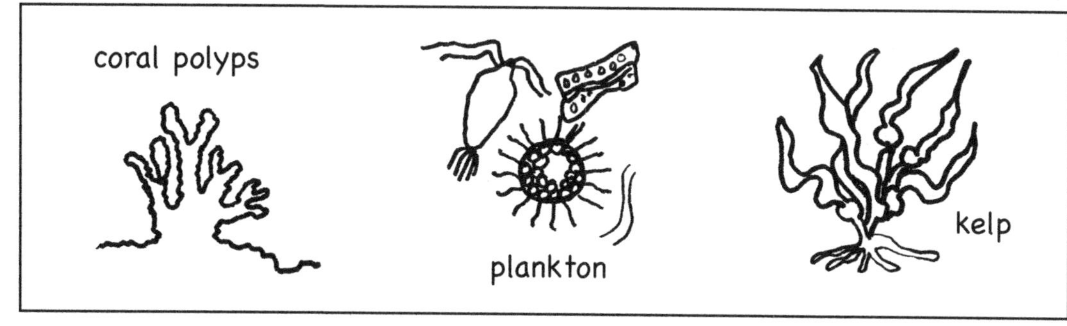

Can you make a food web using these sea creatures by looking at the coral reef marine life table on the next page?

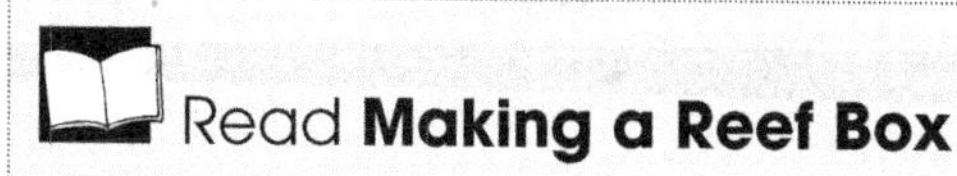

Coral reef marine life

Marine life	Fish	Food
dolphin (mammal)		snapper octopus crabs clownfish
	shark	snapper barramundi octopus butterfly fish
octopus		crab shrimps
	snapper	butterfly fish octopus sea urchins
	barramundi	parrotfish clownfish shrimps
	butterfly fish	coral polyps shrimp
crab		sea urchin shrimp
	clown fish	plankton shrimps coral polyps
	parrotfish	coral algae
shrimp		plankton water fleas
sea urchin		kelp coral polyps
water flea		plankton
coral polyps		sunlight sea water
plankton		decomposed fish
kelp		minerals from soil in the sea

Some unusual reef fish

Cleaner fish

Did you know that some fish are cleaners?

These small **Wrasse** have needle-sharp teeth that can clean the parasites from the mouth, fins and gills of bigger fish. Some big fish will even swim up to the cleaner fish and wait their turn to be cleaned.

Devilfish

This is a small black fish, about 8 cms long, which moves about in a school. Each fish has a pair of lights under its eyes. At night these fish use these lights to see the plankton in the dark water.

Many fish have the same names as other things.

Draw some cartoon pictures of what you think these fish could look like:

trumpetfish	angelfish
batfish	catfish
crocodile fish	squirrelfish
boxfish	butterfly fish
clownfish	lizard fish
hawkfish	goatfish

Make up a game with this table.

1 START →	**2**	**3**	**4**	**5** Caught in net. Go back 3 spaces.	**6** ↓
12	**11**	**10** Dynamite! Go back to start.	**9**	**8**	**7** ←
13 ↓ →	**14**	**15**	**16**	**17**	**18** Hide from shark. Go to 22.
24	**23** You try to eat plastic and get sick. Go back 6 spaces.	**22**	**21**	**20** Eaten! Go back 6 spaces.	**19** ↓ ←
25 ↓ →	**26**	**27** You get speared. Go back to start.	**28**	**29**	**30** ↓
36 You are safely home.	**35**	**34**	**33** You get caught on a hook. Go back 10 spaces.	**32**	**31** ←

Fish game

Here is a game you can play with a friend.

 *Make a small cardboard fish and a dice.*

1 *Throw the dice and move your fish to that number.*

2 *If you land on a box with an instruction you must do what it says.*

3 *The first fish to get to the cave wins the game.*

The water cycle

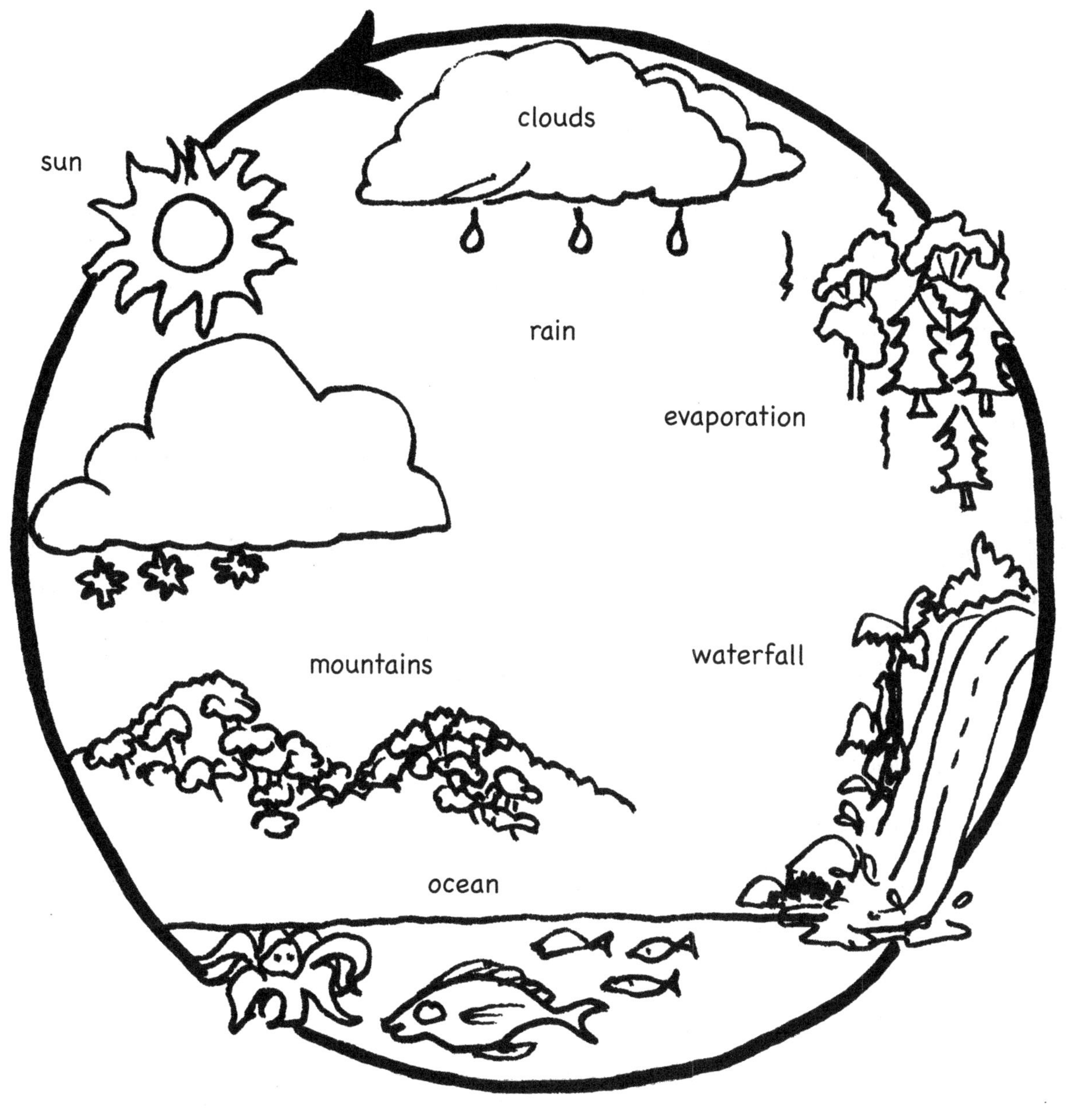

A cycle means that something goes around continuously, like a life cycle.

The sun

The sun shines on the ocean, lakes, streams and rivers and makes them warm. This turns the water into steam or vapour.

Evaporation

The water vapour rises up into the air (it evaporates) and becomes a cloud in the sky.

Condensation

The vapour in the clouds now condenses and turns into water.

Rain

The clouds get so full of water that it starts to rain. The rain falls onto the land and runs into the rivers and lakes and then into the ocean. Some of this waters plants and trees. Some of it soaks down into the ground to make wells.

Oceans

As water flows through rivers, it picks up small amounts of mineral salts from the rocks and soil in the river. This very slightly salty water flows into the oceans and seas. The water in the oceans evaporates, but the salt stays dissolved in the ocean. Salt does not evaporate. When the sun shines, it makes the water warm and turns it into vapour and it becomes cloud again. The cycle starts all over again.

Answer these questions:

1 *What is water vapour?*

2 *What does evaporation mean?*

3 *What does condensation mean?*

4 *How does the sea get salty?*

5 *Where does rain come from?*

Copy the water cycle diagram into your exercise book and label it.

Science experiment: Making your own water cycle

You will need

a large bowl (clear plastic or glass)
plastic wrap
a stone
a smaller container (a cut-down yogurt cup works well)
a rubber band or piece of string

What to do

1. *Put the small container in the middle of the large, clear bowl. Fill the bowl with a little water, being careful not to fill the small container inside.*
2. *Cover the bowl with plastic wrap, and hold the plastic wrap around the rim of the bowl with the rubber band or string.*
3. *Put a stone on top of the plastic wrap in the centre. (See diagram below.)*
4. *Now put it on a windowsill or somewhere where it will get plenty of sun.*

What to look for

How long does it take for water to evaporate and condense on the plastic wrap? Where does the water go after it condenses on the plastic wrap?

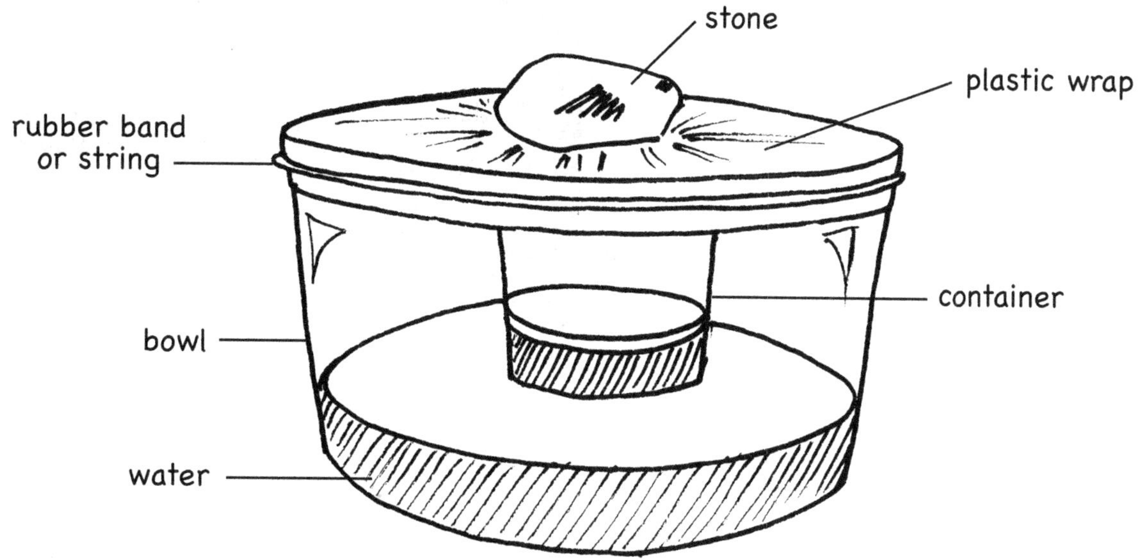

What's happening?

The heat of the sun evaporates the water, which rises, condenses on the cool plastic, and falls into the small container.

Congratulations, you've made a small-scale water cycle!

Making good decisions about our water

Getting water to villages

Adra is a company that has put in 290 water projects and toilets in villages in PNG.

First, a village must have a source (where the water comes from). This is usually a spring in the side of a mountain.

Then a village water committee asks Adra for help to pipe the water to a village storage tank.

Next, the water is filtered and piped to the village. The pipes go to taps. Each tap gives water to 4–5 families.

Finally, when this project is finished, the village water committee must look after it.

Find out how your village gets water. Write a report about your findings.

OR

If you live in a town, find out where the water comes from and write a report about it.

Tell a friend about Adra's water projects.

Use these time signal words to help you: ***first, then, next, finally***.

Water to Port Moresby city

Eda Ranu means "our water" in Motu.

Eda Ranu takes water from Rouna 1, 3, which is a hydro-electric power station on the Laloki River.

This water is pumped through pipes to the water treatment works at Mt Eriama.

The water is treated to make it good to drink, and then it is sent through pipes to houses, schools and factories in Port Moresby.

It comes out of a tap into your house.

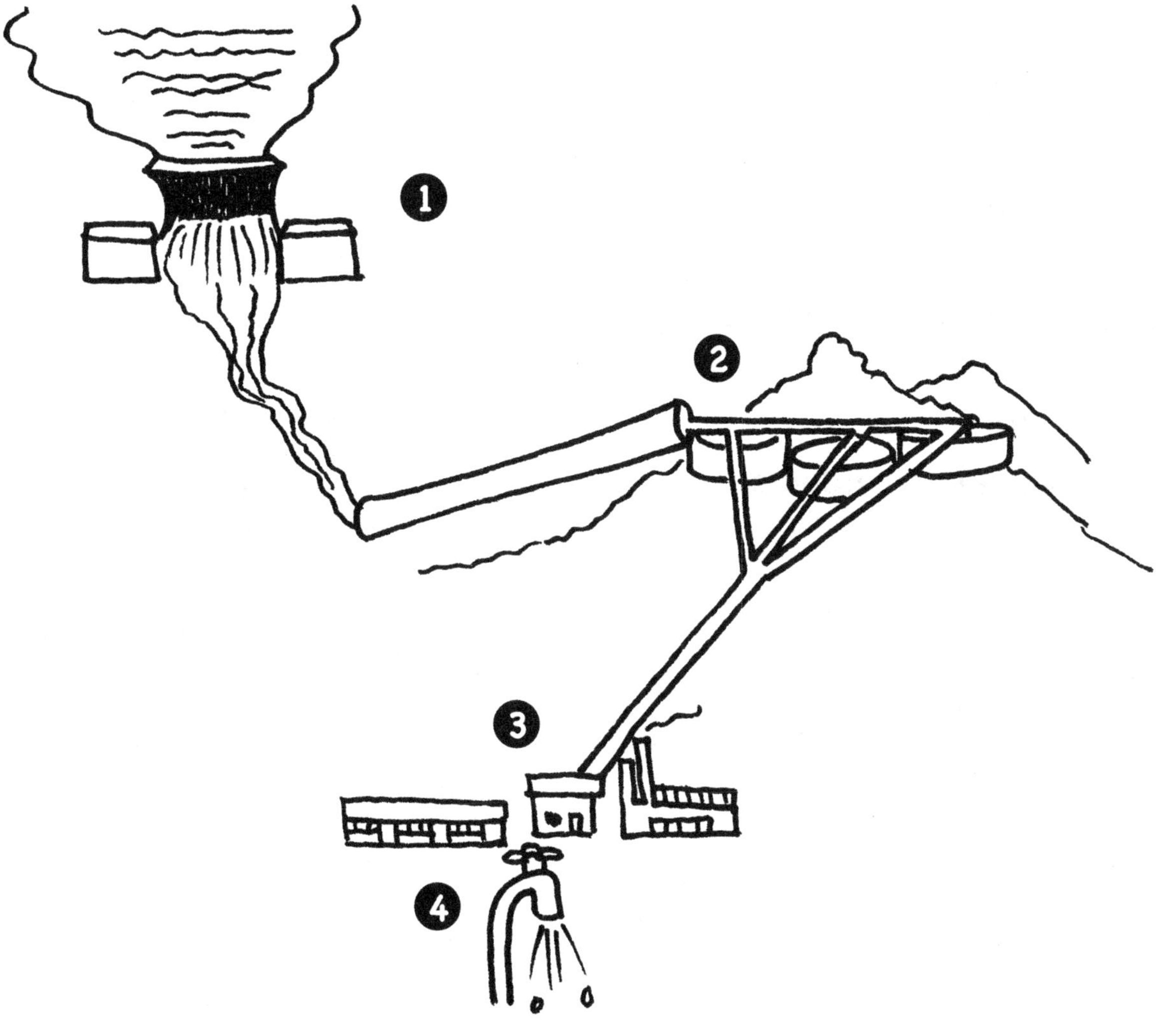

Copy this plan into your book and label it.

4 Making Good Decisions about our Health

Chapter summary

In this chapter you will:

✓ Find out about health services and health products
✓ Learn how to talk to a doctor
✓ Learn about some diseases and how to prevent them
✓ Learn how immunisation helps us
✓ Find out how to be safe in unsafe situations
✓ Learn about food in our community and how to keep it safe
✓ Study the healthy food wheel
✓ Learn about dehydration
✓ Learn about rubbish and how to get rid of it
✓ Find out how to recycle rubbish
✓ Make a poster about drugs, smoking or alcohol.

Cross-curriculum topics

These topics apply only to this chapter.

Topic: Health

Strand: Healthy individuals

Sub-strand: Personal health

5.1.2 Identify causes of common illnesses and take action to promote behaviours that reduce health risks.

Sub-strand: Nutrition

5.1.3 Assess the nutritional value of different foods and take action to promote healthy choices.

Sub-strand: Harmful substances

5.1.4 Evaluate impact of harmful substances on young people and take action to encourage healthy choices.

Strand: Healthy community

Sub-strand: Health services

5.2.1 Identify health services and products in the community and plan ways to assist and care for the services.

Sub-strand: Healthy environment

5.2.2 Assess unsafe situations in the community to reduce harm and promote health.

Topic: Environmental studies

Strand: Caring for my environment

Sub-strand: Managing resources

5.2.1 Design and apply good practices to sustain the environment.

Sub-strand: Managing wastes

5.2.2 Develop and implement action plans to manage waste production and disposal.

Topic: Art

Make a poster.

Make a healthy food wheel.

Health services

Can you find the hospital?

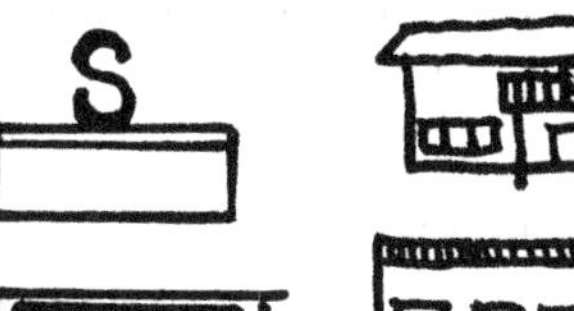

Match the pictures with the type of building.

factory	hotel
house	skyscrapers
shop	church
garage	school
supermarket	hospital

In towns

There are **hospitals** and **clinics** that have doctors and nurses to treat you if you are sick.

In villages

Some church missions have hospitals that will give you health care.

There are **aid posts** and small **health centres** in many places.

These have health workers who are trained only in first aid.

Some village women are trained in family planning and to help women to have babies.

Red Cross

HIV program

The PNG Red Cross HIV program teaches people about HIV and AIDS and supports people who have it.

Helping with natural disasters

The Red Cross helps people who have been injured or lost their homes through natural disasters like floods, tsunamis or earthquakes. They also teach people to prepare for disasters.

Find the ambulance

An ambulance is a special van that takes very sick people to hospital.

It is only used in towns where the roads are good and where a hospital is close by.

Can you find the ambulance?

Match the picture with the name of the vehicle.

police car	4x4	ambulance	van	car
truck	taxi	concrete mixer	PMV	fire engine

Finish these sentences:

1 A taxi is used ______________________________.

2 A car is used ______________________________.

3 A truck is used ______________________________.

4 A fire engine is used ______________________________.

5 A PMV is used ______________________________.

6 A police car is used by ______________ to ______________.

7 An ambulance is used by ______________ to ______________.

8 A 4x4 is used ______________________________.

9 A concrete mixer truck is used ______________________________.

10 A van is used ______________________________.

Giving directions

You are staying with your aunty when she has a heart attack.

You ring the ambulance.

You have to give the ambulance directions **from the hospital** to your aunty's house.

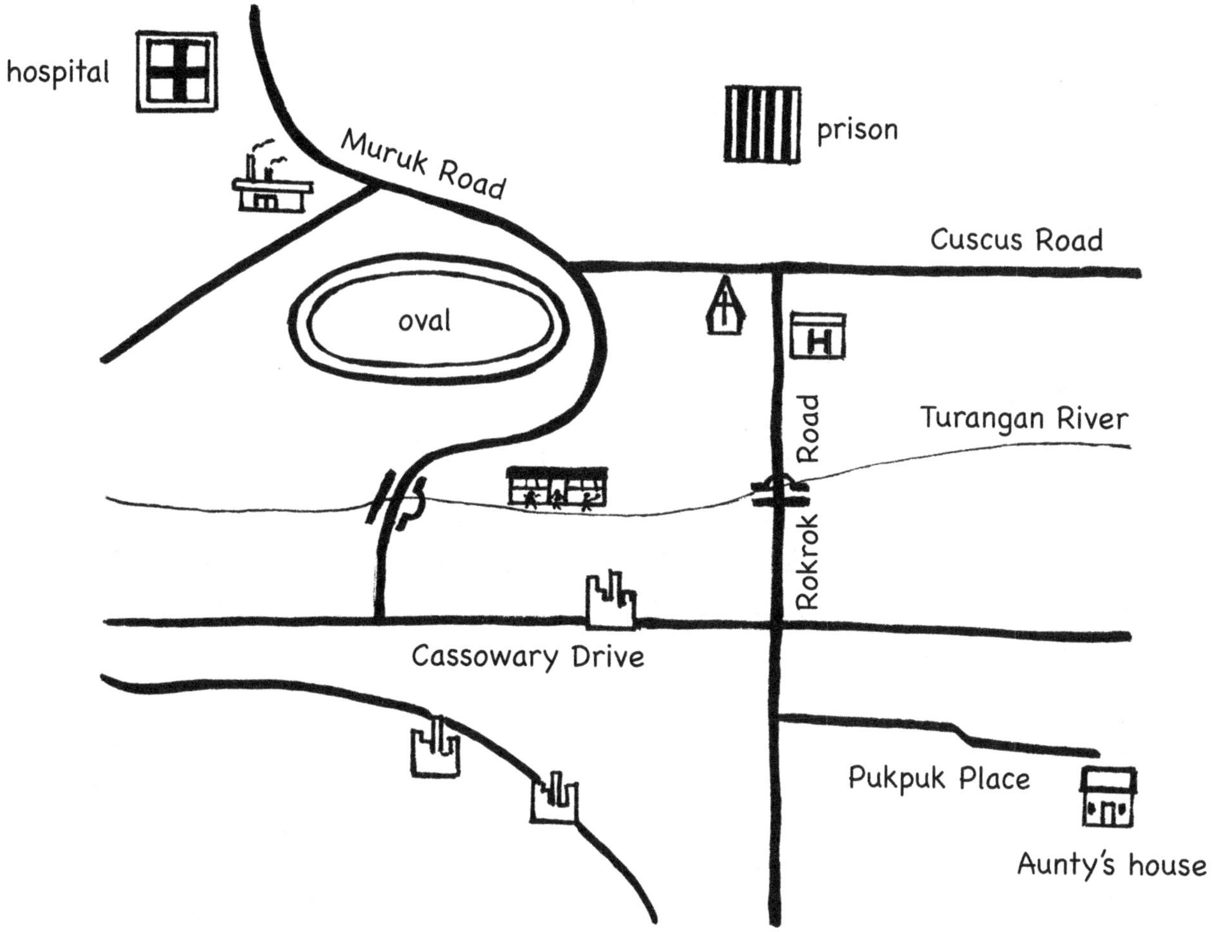

hospital

prison

Muruk Road

Cuscus Road

oval

Turangan River

Rokrok Road

Cassowary Drive

Pukpuk Place

Aunty's house

Start like this:

Go south along Muruk Rd, past the factories, around the oval and **then turn** . . .

____.

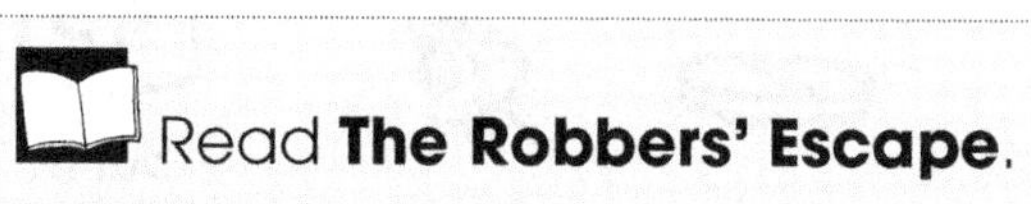
Read **The Robbers' Escape**.

Health products

Health products are available in your community from several places.

Chemist

A chemist is a shop that sells medicines and other things that help us to keep our bodies clean and healthy. First you have to go to a doctor. The doctor will give you a note (**prescription**) to give to the chemist. The chemist will then get the right medicine for you.

For some simple medicines like headache pills, you do not need to see a doctor first.

Trade stores

Some trade stores sell simple medicines.

Traditional medicine

Many traditional medicines are still used in PNG. These are mainly plants.

Some people have been selling dirty water in some towns and saying that it is traditional medicine and that it will cure your sickness. These people are criminals. You must be sure to get traditional medicines only from people you know.

First aid kits

These can be bought from a chemist.

Which of these things would you find inside a first aid kit?

Talking to the doctor

When you or someone else is sick we have to tell the doctor how we feel. He asks us questions to find out what is wrong with us.

What happened, Kali?

I fell over onto my ankle.

Does it hurt?

Yes, it really hurts.

I think you've sprained your ankle. I'll put on a bandage.

Thanks, Doctor. That feels better already.

Draw a cartoon like the picture above. Draw a doctor or a nurse with a patient.

Choose from the phrases below to set out questions and answers like on page 99. You can use each phrase more than once.

1. What's wrong?
2. What happened?
3. I have a headache.
4. I cut myself.
5. We need an ambulance.
6. I hit my head and I feel dizzy.
7. I fell and hurt my leg.
8. Does it hurt when I touch it?
9. I have a bad cough.
10. How do you feel?
11. I'll give you some pills to take.
12. We have to stop the bleeding.
13. Have you been sick?
14. Did you eat something bad?
15. I'll take your temperature.
16. I'll give you an injection.
17. You need to drink plenty of water.
18. Take this medicine twice a day.
19. My throat is sore.
20. My stomach aches.
21. Where does it hurt?
22. I have a fever.
23. I feel sick.
24. Poke out your tongue.
25. Thank you, Doctor.
26. I ate some seafood.
27. Where is it sore?
28. I think it's broken.
29. It's sore right here.
30. You'll need a splint.
31. I'll rub on ointment.
32. You need a plaster.
33. Yes.
34. I don't feel well.
35. I have diarrhoea.
36. Right here.
37. I think you have food poisoning.
38. I think you have malaria.
39. Lie down and rest.

Diseases

Our bodies get sick for many different reasons.

Sometimes we may be sick for just a short time, but sometimes we may have a disease, which is a bad sickness.

Different diseases have different **symptoms** (things that go wrong with our bodies).

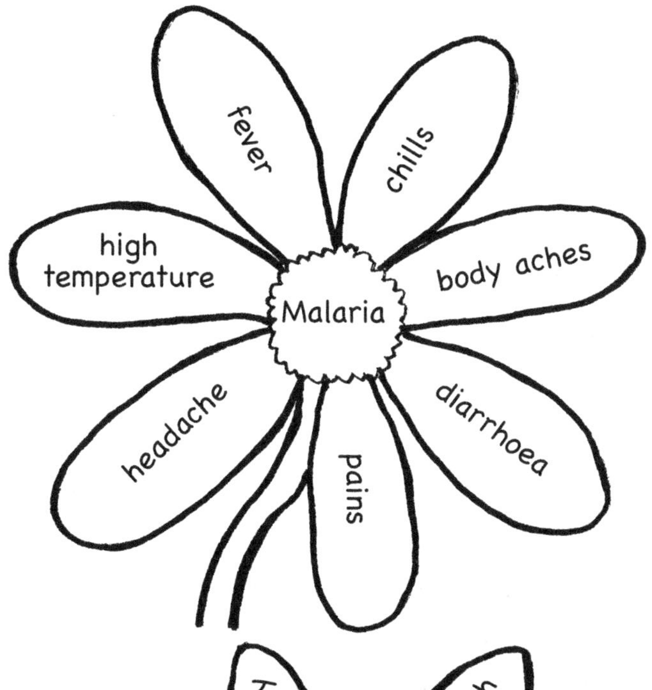

Cause: Malaria is caused by a mosquito.

Cure: Get medicine from an aid post or clinic.

Prevention: Sleep under a mosquito net.

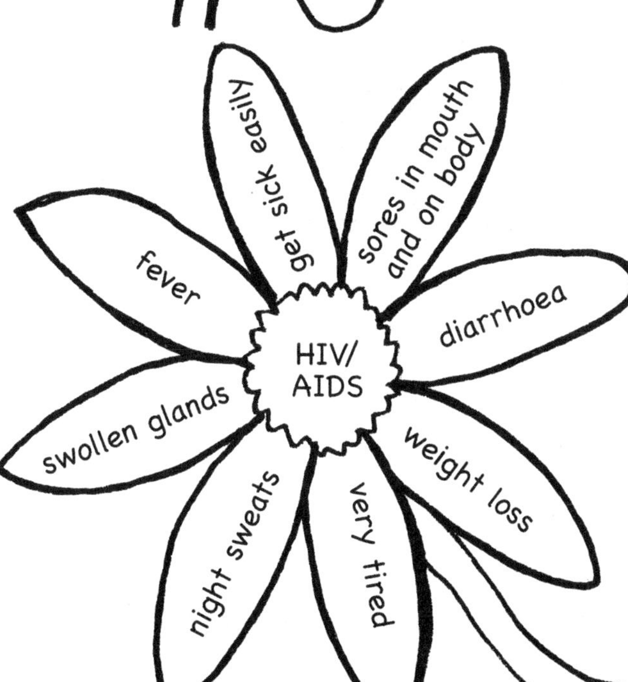

Cause: HIV is passed on by body fluids.

Cure: There is no cure for AIDS. Some medicines help.

Prevention: When you are an adult, do not have sex with lots of people.

Cause means why you get the sickness.

Cure means how to fix it.

Prevention means how to not get sick.

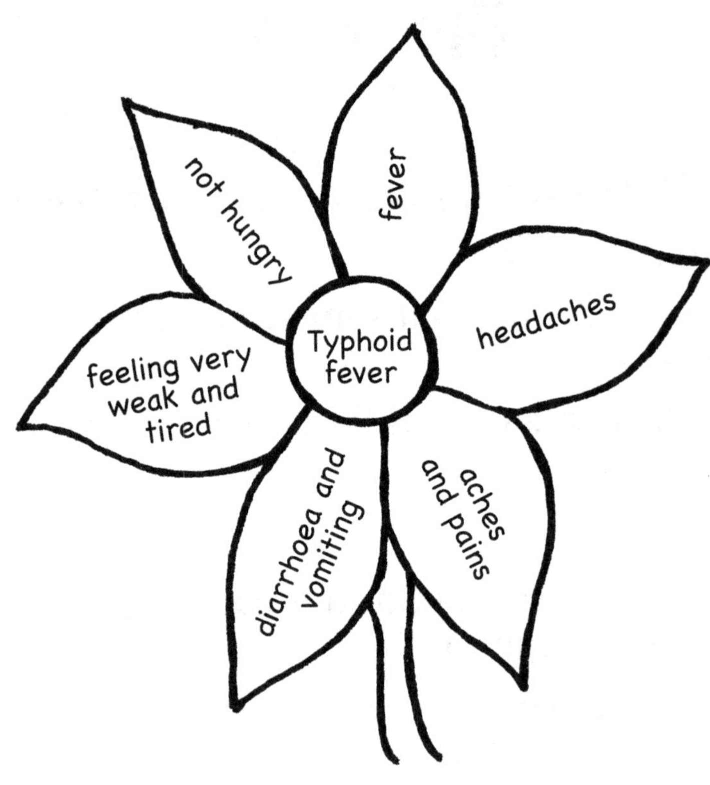

Cause: Germs in bad food or water.

Cure: See the doctor to get antibiotic drugs.

Prevention: Keep chicken in the fridge. Don't eat old food that has gone bad or drink dirty water.

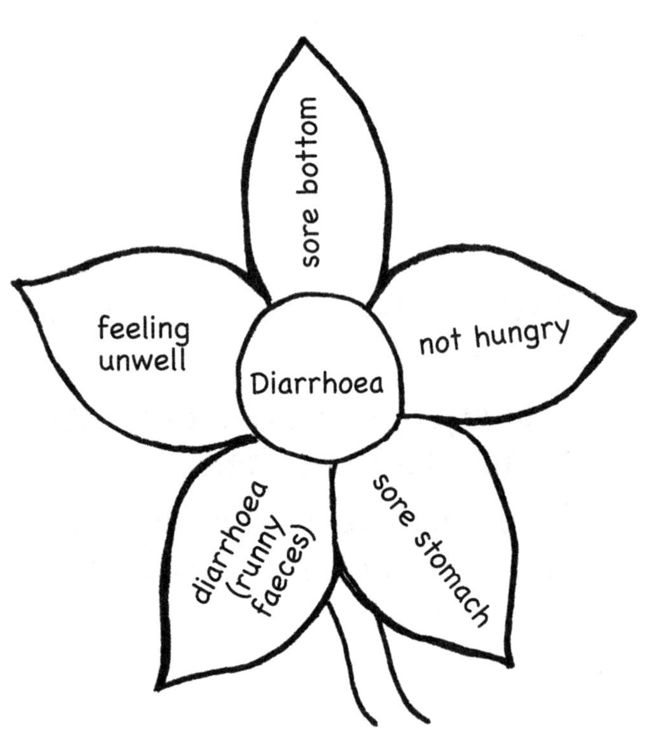

Cause: Germs on dirty hands.

Cure: Drink lots of water with salt in it.

Prevention: Wash your hands after using the toilet and before handling food. Make sure your drinking water is safe to drink.

If you or your family have these ***symptoms****, you should go to a hospital to see a doctor.*

You be the doctor

This man is very sick. You are the doctor. He tells you his symptoms. Can you say what's wrong with him?

Immunisation

Immunisation means to get an injection that will stop you getting a disease.

Many children in PNG are immunised against bad diseases.

In 2006, 100 children died from a sickness called measles.

Only 30% of the children in the Western Highlands were immunised against measles. This could be why so many died.

Write a letter to your mother explaining what immunisation means and saying why the children in your family should be immunised.

Preventing disease

To keep healthy we must do these things.

Eat healthy food

What?

Wash our hands

When?

Keep our bodies clean

How?

Drink lots of water

Why?

Sleep under a mosquito net

Why?

Keep our house clean

How?

Keep our clothes clean

How?

Keep our teeth clean

Why?

Write a paragraph about each of the above, explaining how you would do these things.

Answer the question under each heading.

Unsafe situations in the community

Rivers, sea, swamps

These areas can be unsafe in many ways.

Look at this picture and write down four dangers to people living by the river.

Water sources

Look at this picture and write down three dangers to people living by this water source.

Busy roads

Look at this picture and write down three dangers to people.

Dumped rubbish

Look at this picture and write three sentences about what should be done with rubbish and why.

 Read **Madman Mooti**.

Bush toilets

Write a sentence saying why bush toilets can be harmful. How can we keep them safe?

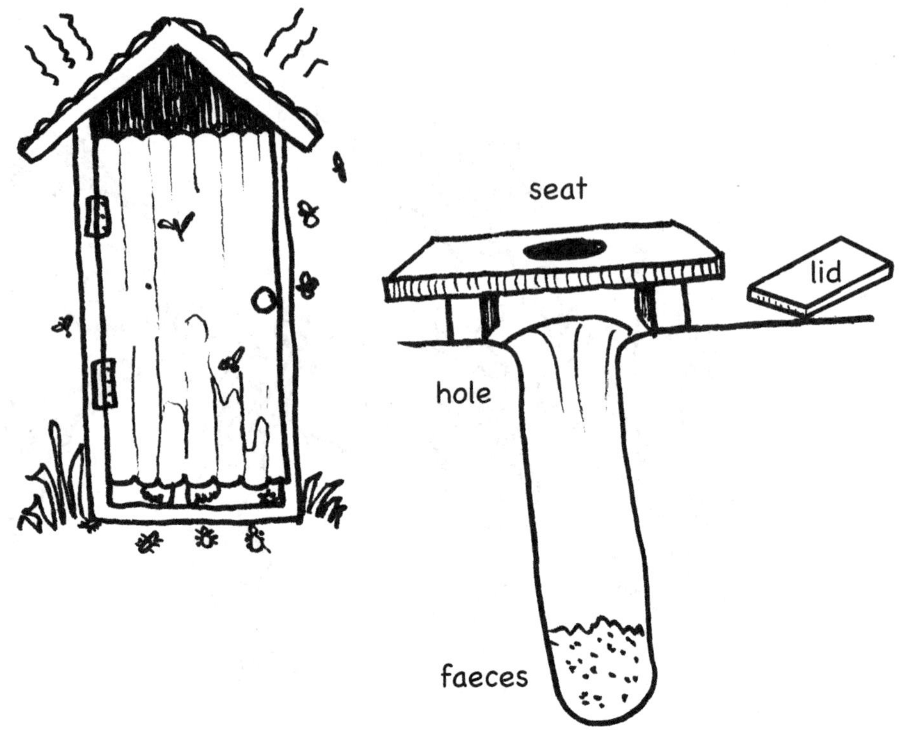

Unclean areas

If there is a dirty area in your community, what are three things that you should do?

Old buildings in disrepair

 *If a building is broken or dangerous, what should you do?*

Overloaded vehicles/boats

 *Look at this picture and write about the dangers of overloaded boats or PMVs.*

Flood areas

If you live near a river, you may get flooded. What should you do if this happens?

Bushfires

You should not light fires in the bush. If the bush is dry, it will burn easily and you might start a forest fire. Why is a bushfire dangerous?

Keeping food safe

Food can easily go bad in a hot climate.

Some food, such as milk, butter, fish and meat, goes bad quickly.

If you have a fridge, keep those things and your fruit and vegetables there.

Keep all other food in a cool place that is safe from rats and insects.

Preserving food

Drying

Food can be dried very slowly in an oven. This keeps it from going bad. Proper storage stops insects and rats from eating food. It also keeps it dry so that it doesn't go bad.

Which foods could be dried?

bananas taro pawpaw sugar cane

Smoking

Food can be kept longer if it is smoked.

Which foods could be smoked?

pineapple fish cabbage beef

Freezing

If you have a freezer at home, most food can be frozen and kept for a long time. When you want to eat it, you just take it out of the freezer and let it thaw. Then you cook it the way you normally would.

Which foods could be frozen?

potatoes kaukau mango juice chicken

Food in our community

The type of food we eat often depends on where we live.

This is Kipa. He lives in the Western Province of PNG.

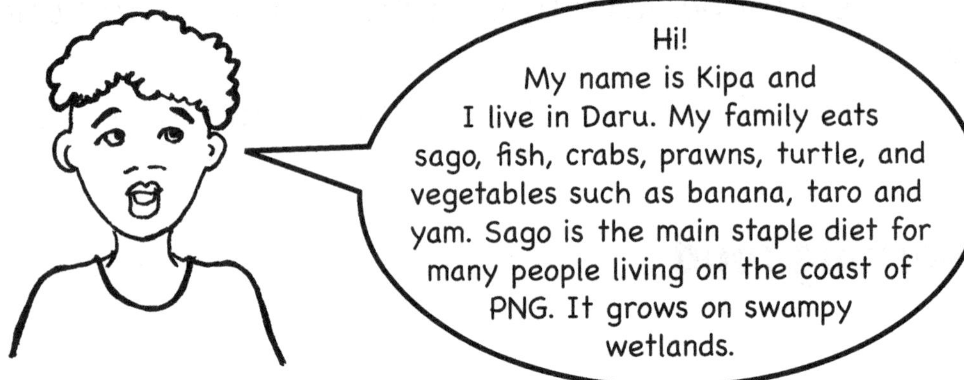

Can you say the English names for these?

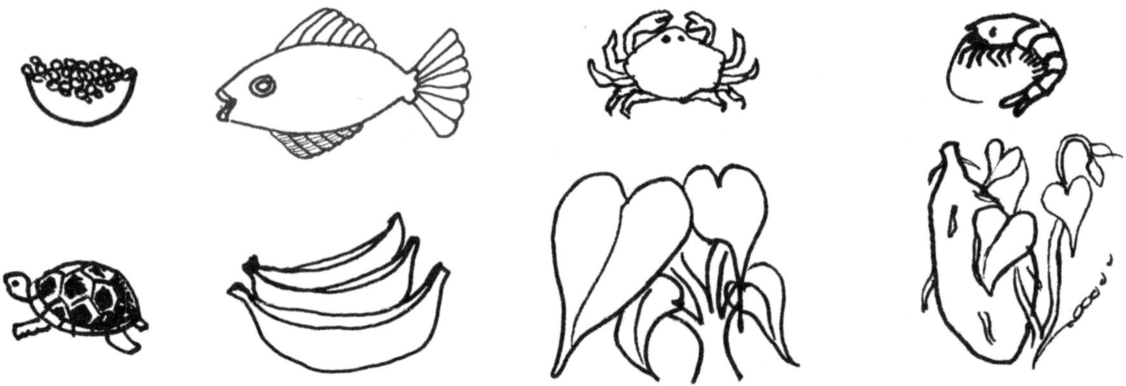

This is how we make the sago:

- The sago tree is cut down.
- We cut away the bark and get out the pith of the tree. We scratch it up and mash it into sawdust.
- Next we put it on a palm leaf and put it on woven palm leaves to squeeze it and wash it. The strained water then becomes the sago. The sago settles out of the water.

 *Write a story saying how you prepare your main food.*

Draw a box like the ones above and draw yourself in it. Write down in a speech bubble where you live and what you eat. What is your staple food?

Do you eat much Western food? If so, what kind?

Healthy food wheel

We need to eat different types of food each day to keep healthy.

- **Carbohydrates:** These give us energy.
- **Protein:** These help our bodies to grow and repair themselves.
- **Fats:** These give us energy.
- **Vitamins:** These keep us healthy.
- **Mineral salts:** These keep our teeth, bones and muscles healthy.
- **Fibre:** These keep our intestines healthy.

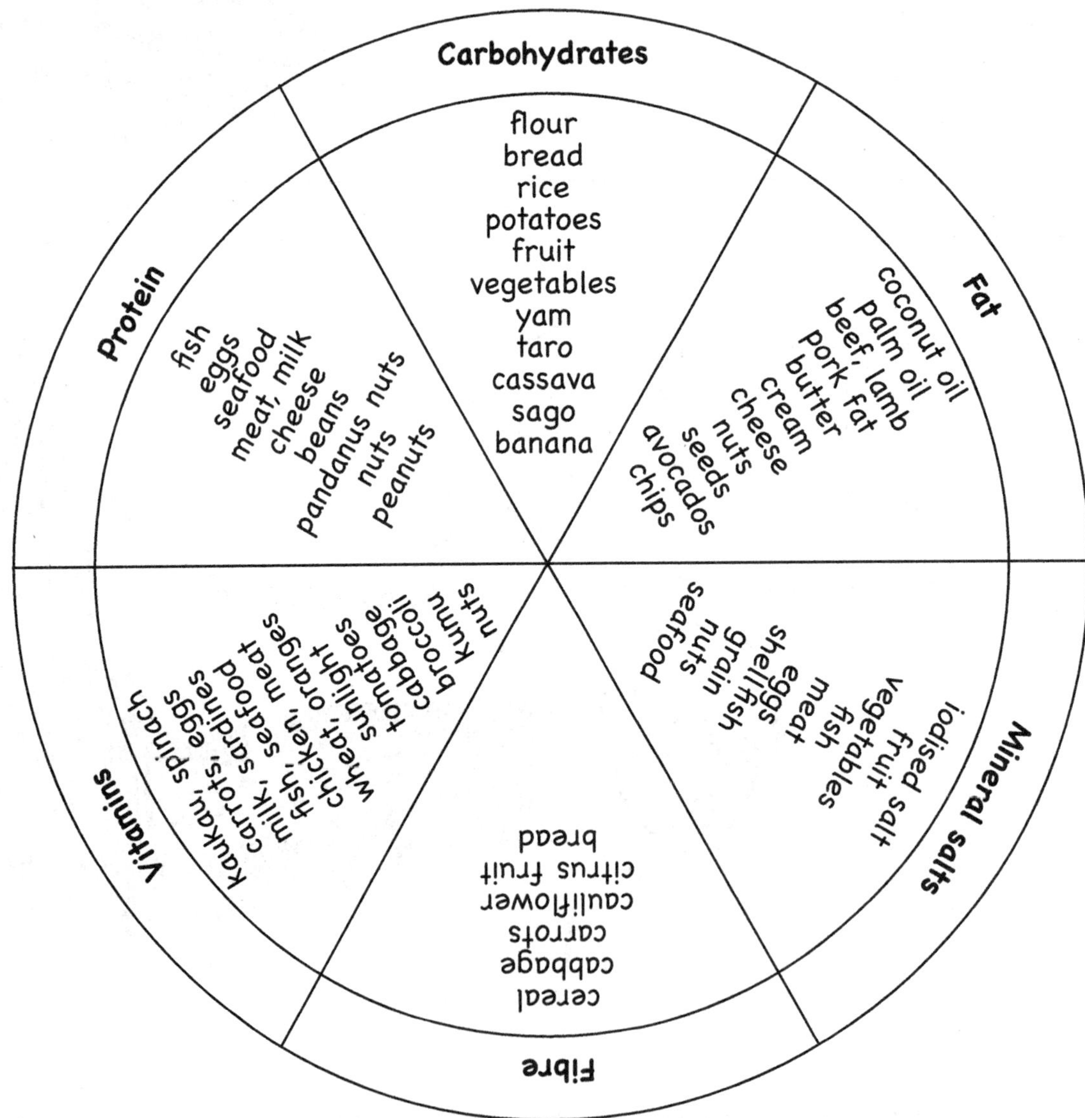

Copy this wheel into your book.

Underline all the foods you normally eat each week.

Food values

When you buy food, you need to look at the label on the tin or packet to find out what the **food value** is in that food. We also need to look at the expiry date to see how old it is. If the food is out of date, don't buy it!

Remember that fresh food is much healthier than tinned or packaged food.

We measure the food value in units:

1000 milligrams = 1 gram

g = grams

mg = milligrams

One serving is about 100 g.

Per serving:

Protein 10.8 g

Fat 10.8 g

Carbohydrate 34.4 g

Sugars 16.1 g

Fibre 11.9 g

Salt 1000 mg

Iron 2.7 mg

Are baked beans good to eat? Why?

Per serving:

Protein 2.5 g

Fat 0.2 g

Carbohydrates 29.0 g

Sugars 0 g

Sodium (salt) 2 mg

Potassium 80 mg

Is rice good to eat? Why?

Per serving:

Protein 4.6 g

Fat 10.7 g

Carbohydrate 25.0 g

Sugar 19.7 g

Sodium (salt) 53.8 mg

1. *Which of these foods gives you the most energy?*
2. *Which food has the most sugar?*
3. *Which is the most fattening?*
4. *Which food has the most protein?*
5. *Which food is very salty?*
6. *Which food is good to eat a lot of because it has no sugar, low salt and fat but gives you energy?*

For you to do

Look at the food in the picture. Find out what the food value is in each food, or in food like it.

Write a report on each food saying whether it is a healthy food or not. Say why.

packet of biscuits

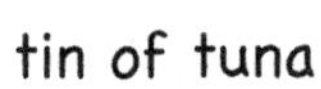

tin of tuna

bag of lollies

tinned meat

cake of chocolate

packet of potato chips

Read **Dinosaurs in PNG?**

Dehydration

Dehydration means that your body needs more water.

Signs of dehydration are:

- feeling dizzy or light-headed
- dry mouth and lips
- heart beating fast
- dark or strong-smelling urine.

What makes us dehydrated?

Look at the pictures and choose the activities that would make you dehydrated.

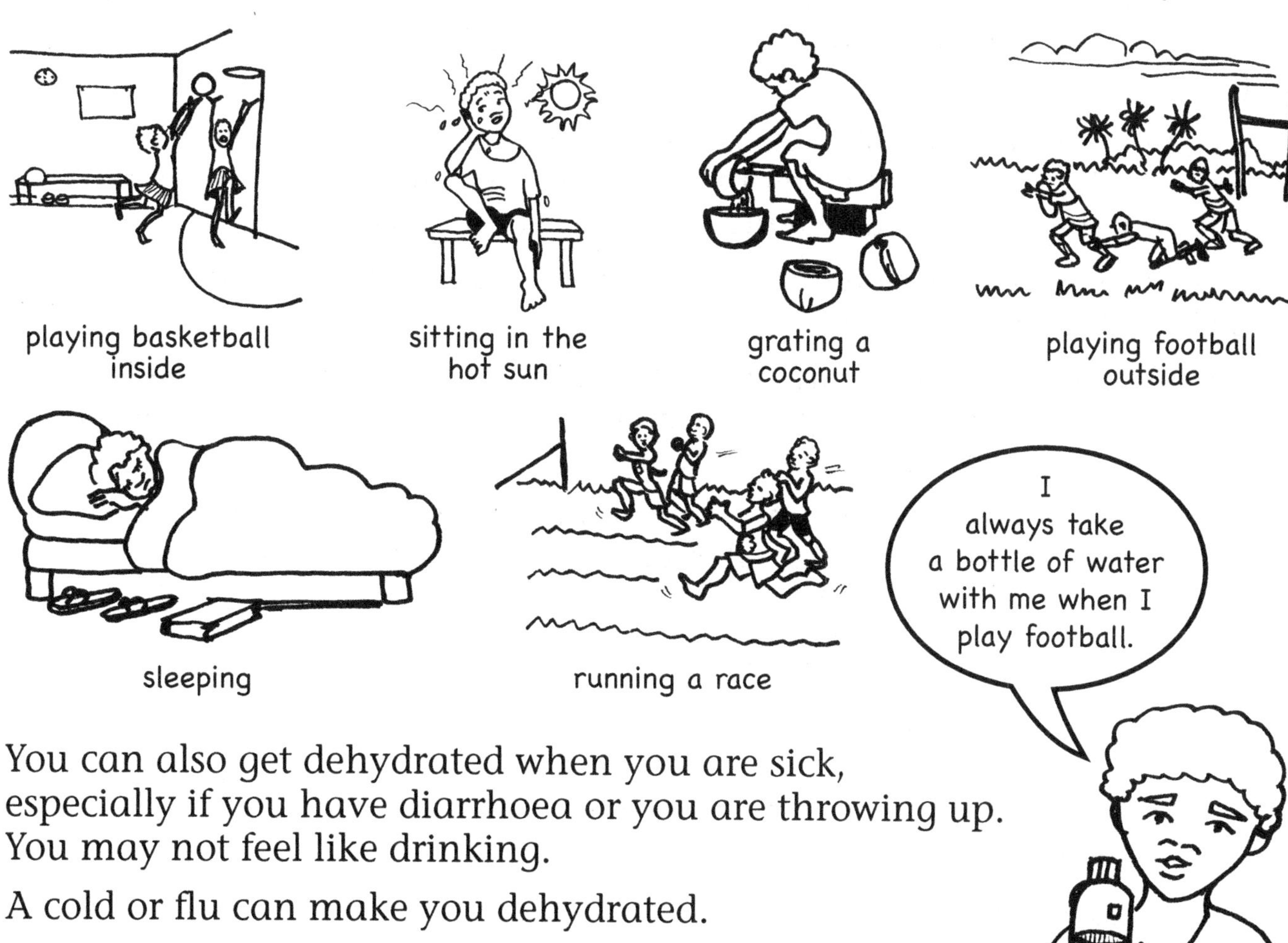

You can also get dehydrated when you are sick, especially if you have diarrhoea or you are throwing up. You may not feel like drinking.

A cold or flu can make you dehydrated.

Remember to drink lots of clean water if you're sick or have a bad headache.

Looking after our environment

This speech was made by Sir Michael Somare for World Environment Day in 2005. Read it carefully.

We have a beautiful country but everywhere you look around in our towns you see plastic bags, red betel-nut stains and graffiti. We take for granted our surroundings and environment.

To plan and prepare for a better future we must get rid of some of these bad habits. We must change the attitude that it is the concern of the city councils only. This is our country and we must feel responsible for its health and wellbeing.

It is also the responsibility of the community to ensure that bushfires are not lit in the dry season. Papua New Guineans are prone to respiratory illnesses and air pollution from fires affects the health of everyone in the community.

Last but not least, we all need oxygen to breathe. Trees provide that essential ingredient. While many of our people still use wood to cook, it is very important to also replace the trees that you are chopping down.

Trees release oxygen and absorb the carbon dioxide that is in the air, giving us cleaner air to breathe.

We all have our part to play in the preservation and conservation of the environment. Nature has given so much to us and we must give back to her by looking after our environment.

In order to achieve this balance the community must work together. We should not leave the issue of environment for just the government to resolve.

Answer these questions:

1 *What type of pollution is seen around the towns?*

2 *Why are bushfires bad?*

3 *Why do we need trees?*

4 *What should we do if we cut down a tree?*

5 *What is your responsibility to the environment?*

Getting rid of rubbish

Rubbish brings rats and disease. It also smells bad and looks untidy.

A place where rubbish is dumped is called a rubbish dump or a tip.

In 1997, the Six Mile Dump at Port Moresby was closed because it was full. Another one was opened – the Baruni Dump.

Dump problems

- People lived there (squatters).
- People fought over who should live there.
- Squatters got sick. Some died of cancer.
- Some children born there had birth defects.
- Some people drank poison out of nearly empty bottles.
- Marijuana was sold there. People became drug addicts.
- There was air pollution from gases in the dump.

 *Write a report about the problems in the dump.*

 *Find out what happens to rubbish in your area.*

Beach rubbish

1 Many villages around Port Moresby have their houses built over the

_______________ .

2 Many children swim in the water below which is filled with sewage and

_______________ .

3 Sewage is _______________ waste.

4 People still catch and eat fish from this water, which makes the people

_______________ .

5 The _______________ from this is awful.

6 The worst time of the year is between November and January, when there is no _______________.

7 The sea is changing colour because it is full of bacteria (_______________).

8 This is called _______________.

rubbish	sick	wind	pollution
water	human	smell	germs

I am from Pari Village. I have lived here all my life. I think that the cutting down of mangroves, as well as all the rubbish in the Taurama area, has made the tuna disappear. They used to come to this area at certain times of the year to spawn. The tuna rituals that were practised by our people for years have now been lost. I am very sad about this.

North of Pari Village, the shoreline is covered in rubbish after years of dumping. The current used to clean this area but now it's all clogged up. We have to do something!

Draw a table and put the rubbish in this picture under these headings to show how to get rid of it.

- *dump*
- *bury*
- *burn*
- *recycle*

What do you think can be done about the shoreline rubbish problem?

Rules for recycling

1. Reduce

This means to make it smaller.

2. Reuse

This means to use it again.

3. Repair

This means to fix it, instead of throwing it away.

4. Recycle

This means to make it into something else.

Can you give examples of these?

Can you think of other things you could recycle?

Find the words hidden in the puzzle.

p	g	l	a	s	s	p	y	m	b
l	b	f	m	c	c	n	j	c	o
a	p	a	p	e	r	a	h	r	t
s	p	g	o	g	a	b	o	u	t
t	i	n	s	g	p	u	l	s	l
i	t	d	s	y	a	e	e	e	e
c	g	p	w	e	p	n	u	s	s
r	u	b	b	i	s	h	b	i	n

bottles
glass
tins
paper
scrap
rubbish bin
pit
hole
plastic

Taurama legend

Many years ago in the Taurama area, near Pari Village, a woman gave birth to five fishes in the mangroves.

These fish were tuna or kidukidu.

The woman would go to the mangroves every morning and bang two sticks together to call them so that she could feed them.

The husband wondered what had happened to her baby, and so one morning he followed her to the mangroves.

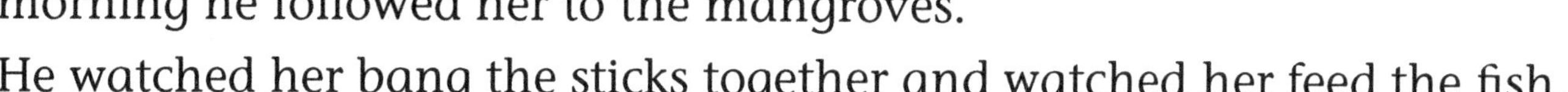

He watched her bang the sticks together and watched her feed the fish.

When she had gone home, he banged the sticks together and caught one of the fish when it came up to him. He killed it and ate it.

When the wife found out what had happened, she told her remaining fish children to go out to sea and only come in to spawn (lay eggs).

From that time on, the people of Pari Village have their own rituals (customs) for how to catch tuna.

1 *What did the woman give birth to?*

2 *Is this the truth? Why?*

3 *How did the woman call the fish?*

4 *How did the husband find out about the fish?*

5 *How did he catch one of the fish?*

6 *What did the woman tell the remaining fish to do? Why?*

7 *What is another name for fish eggs?*

8 *What is a ritual?*

Write this legend in your own words.

Draw your own picture about it.

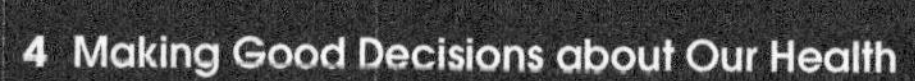

Drugs

Read this poster.

DO HUGS

NOT DRUGS

Talk about this poster. What things is it telling you that the words don't tell you? How does it make you feel?

Design your own poster warning people about drugs, smoking, drinking or AIDS.